Napoleon Hill has given the key to success and happiness to millions of readers. And he has given it in simple, down-to-earth language that anyone can understand easily.

The world's foremost scholar and thinker in the science of human success, he has uncovered the essential secret of those fortunate people who are masters of their own fates. Success is not a cold and grim business—it is a warm, gratifying, thrilling, and miraculous way of living that anyone can attain.

At an early age, Napoleon Hill began to meet and study great achievers—Andrew Carnegie, Henry Ford, Thomas A. Edison, Cyrus H. K. Curtis II, F. W. Woolworth, Theodore Roosevelt, Alexander Graham Bell, William Howard Taft, Luther Burbank, Woodrow Wilson, and Franklin D. Roosevelt.

In each of these men he perceived the miracle-working power of the personality that is conditioned for success.

You Can Work Your Own Miracles

Napoleon Hill

FAWCETT GOLD MEDAL • NEW YORK

CONTENTS

You Can Work
Your Own Miracles

Prologue

Every adversity, every unpleasant circumstance, every failure, and *every physical pain* carries with it *the seed of an equivalent benefit*. Ralph Waldo Emerson's greatest essay, "Compensation," confirms this truth in elaborate detail; and I have just passed through an experience that not only confirms it but has provided the means by which I may help millions of people convert physical pain into a constructive interlude of great benefit to themselves.

I was sitting in a dentist's chair in Los Angeles, California, waiting for him to extract the last nine of my teeth, preparatory to fitting temporary dentures. My dentist had anesthetized both my upper and lower jaws and was waiting, as I thought, for the anesthetic to take effect. Every minute or so he inserted an instrument into my mouth and appeared to be examining my gums. After this had been going on for a while, I asked, "Doctor, aren't you about ready to begin pulling my teeth?"

With a look of astonishment on his face, he replied, "What do you mean by that question? I have them all out but three. There they are, on the table in front of you."

I looked, and sure enough, six of my teeth had been extracted without my knowing the operation was going on. Then followed a conversation between my dentist and myself which yielded to me the "seed of an equivalent benefit" as compensation for the dental surgery I had undergone. It may well benefit millions of people who will read my story and take advantage of the lesson it affords when they visit their dentists. That "seed" consisted in the plan and purpose of this volume, which were inspired by that conversation.

As the last three teeth had been extracted my dentist inquired, "Where were you while I was pulling six of your teeth?"

"Out at Radio Station KFWB," I replied, "rehearsing my next Sunday broadcast."

"Well," my dentist exclaimed, "I have been practicing dentistry for thirty years, but I have never before had a patient sit in my chair and have teeth extracted without knowing it. How in the world could you do it?"

"That was easy enough," I answered. "I conditioned my mind for this operation before you started it. Part of that conditioning consisted of my complete disassociation from it, by concentrating my mind on something pleasant and far removed from the operation itself."

"Man alive!" returned my dentist. "If you know how to teach others to condition their minds for dental work, so as to take the fear out of dentistry, and you will publish your formula in a book, the dentists of this country will help you sell a million copies within a year."

Before I left my dentist's office that day I had planned this volume and outlined the entire method by which I had converted the fear of dentistry into a magnificent interlude which may bring to millions of people the formula for mastery of physical pain.

A strange feature of this formula is that it is based upon the same method by which I have helped millions of people condition their minds for material prosperity. The formula has been more than fifty years in the making. It was begun when Andrew Carnegie commissioned me to organize the world's first practical philosophy of individual achievement, and its refinement has come from the personal experiences of more than five hundred of America's top-ranking successful people who collaborated with me in perfecting that philosophy.

Before I can hand over the formula it will be necessary for me to help the reader condition his or her mind to receive it. Just as one must master the fundamentals of elementary mathematics before going on to higher mathematics, so must one acquire the knowledge of mind-conditioning step by step, by studying the important subjects which are related to this knowledge, as set forth in the chapters which follow.

By patiently and thoughtfully following me through the pages of this volume, you may find a new world of riches you did not know you possessed. I shall describe, in plain language anyone can understand, the formula which helped me convert dental surgery into a magnificent interlude entirely free from pain.

But that is only the starter!

The system of mind-conditioning I shall reveal in this book will aid one in mastering many circumstances of life he does not desire, such as physical pain, sorrow, fear, and despair. It will also prepare him to acquire the things which are desired, such as peace of mind, self-understanding, financial prosperity and harmony in all human relations.

This volume is far and away the most revealing, in terms of utter frankness, of many subjects which I have left out of my previous books, because I desired to present them under the auspices of dentists and physicians whose patients need most of the information they convey.

In my previous books I have shown how to make one's job, profession, or business pay off in profitable terms, and it has been estimated that my books have helped millions of people become financially prosperous. In this volume I have aimed to help people make LIFE pay off in terms of their own choice, through a system of self-discipline which has the astounding advantage of being subject to proof of its soundness by every reader of this volume.

Lastly, I have written this book for people who have personal problems they have not solved and unpleasant circumstances they must master, with the hope that it will be of great benefit to every person who reads it, and reflect credit on my physician and dentist friends who may recommend it to their patients.

At the beginning I only planned to write a book which would help people condition their minds for dentistry or surgery, but as I began to outline the skeleton of the book's contents, I envisioned a much greater purpose than the original—a purpose which would give the reader the full benefit of more than forty years of research into the causes of both success and failure, happiness and misery; important knowledge I accumulated while organizing the Science of Success, which now appears under many different titles, with a reader following throughout most of the world.

In the chapters which follow I shall introduce some of the great miracles of life through which my readers may discover and appropriate the Twelve Great Riches described in a subsequent chapter. I shall also reveal the means by which fear, poverty, sorrow, failure, and physical pain may be transmuted into inspirational forces of great benefit.

Read with an open mind the chapters which follow and you shall have revealed to you the greatest of all miracles— one that I cannot describe because it is known only to you, and it is *entirely under your control*! This miracle is one which contains a password capable of making you free and helping you appropriate all of the Twelve Great Riches of Life. It can bring you peace of mind and give you a well-balanced life, consisting of every circumstance and every material thing you need or desire.

In this volume, I have given you, through the description of the miracles, one half of the password; but the other half is in your possession and must be added to the half I have provided. As you read these chapters, the half in your possession will be revealed to you. And when you recognize it, appropriate it, and begin to transmute it into a full life of your own making. *You will understand that this volume has given you something much more important than the way to remove the fear of physical pain from dentistry and surgery.*

And having thus become the master of *a few simple things*, you shall become also the master of *still greater things*.

—Napoleon Hill

CHAPTER I

Everyone Can Perform "Miracles"

An expectant father was pacing up and down the hall in front of the operating room at the hospital, waiting to hear whether it was a boy or a girl.

The door opened, two nurses came out and passed by the waiting father without looking in his direction. Then the doctor came to the door, hesitated a moment, and motioned the impatient father to enter.

"Before you go in," the doctor began, "I must prepare you for a shock. It's a boy and he was born without ears. He hasn't the slightest sign of ears, and of course he will be deaf all his life."

"He may have been born without ears," the father exclaimed, "but he will not go through life deaf!"

"Now don't become excited," returned the doctor. "But you may as well prepare yourself to accept the conditions as they are; not as you wish them to be. Medical science has known of other cases like that of your son, but not one of the children born in his condition ever learned to hear."

"Doctor, I have great respect for your skill as a physician, but I am also a doctor in a certain sense, for I have discovered a powerful remedy sufficient for human needs in practically every circumstance. The first step one must take in applying this remedy is to refuse to accept as inevitable any circumstance one does not desire, *and I am notifying you, here and now, that I shall never accept my son's affliction as something which cannot be corrected.*"

The doctor made no reply, but the look of astonishment on his face clearly said, "You poor fellow, I feel sorry for you, but you'll find out there are some circumstances of life which one is forced to accept." He took the father by the arm and walked into the room where the mother and child awaited him, turned back the spread and stood silently while the father looked at what the doctor sincerely believed to be one of those "circumstances of life which one is forced to accept."

Time moved onward rapidly. Twenty-five years later another doctor smilingly emerged from his laboratory with some X-rays in his hands. "Miraculous," he exclaimed, "I have X-rayed this young man's head from every possible angle and I see no evidence that he possesses any form of hearing equipment. Yet my tests show that he has sixty-five percent of his normal hearing capacity."

The doctor was a well-known ear specialist of New York City, and the X-rays he held in his hands were made of the head of the young man who doubtless would have gone through life deaf had it not been for the intervention of a father who refused to accept that condition and who did something to cause nature to correct it.

I can vouch for the correctness of these statements because I am the father who refused to accept as incurable even so great an affliction as that of being born without ears.

For almost nine years I devoted a major portion of my time to the application of a power which finally restored to my son sixty-five percent of his normal hearing. It was sufficient to enable him to go through the grade school, high school, and college with grades that equaled the best of students. And it was sufficient to enable him to adjust himself to life so as to live normally and without inconveniences or embarrassment such as most deaf persons suffer.

How was this "miracle" performed?

Who or what did the performing, and what took place inside the head of the child born without ears which enabled him to develop sufficient hearing capacity to carry him through life satisfactorily?

These same questions were put to the ear specialist. Here is his reply: "Without doubt, the psychological directives the father gave through the child's subconscious mind influenced nature to improvise some sort of a nerve system which connected the brain with the inner walls of the skull, and enabled the boy to hear by what is now known as bone conduction."

It is hoped that by the time the reader shall have finished reading this volume the exact nature of the "miracle" which saved a child from going through life as a deaf person will be revealed. That is the major purpose in writing the book.

The author has been aided by this "miracle" ever since he first became conscious of it, when he was quite a young man. It has helped him to master fear, superstition, ignorance, and poverty, the four enemies of mankind to which so many people yield without a fight because they do not understand how to apply the "miracle" in refusing to accept from Life that which *they do not want*.

The exact nature of the "miracle" is something one person cannot describe to another until that person has been mentally conditioned to receive it. For this reason it may be necessary for the reader to read and analyze all of the subsequent chapters of this book before he is conditioned to receive the full meaning of the "miracle."

Some very definite clues have been described in this

chapter, but they may not be sufficient to reveal the supreme secret by which one may successfully reject from Life that which one does not desire.

This secret is worthy of earnest search because it is the master key that will unlock the doors to multiple blessings for all who possess it, including the mastery of dread of dental and medical surgery.

The mental attitude in which you read this book will determine, to a large extent, the time and the place in the book where the secret may be revealed to you. Therefore, let us turn our attention to some of the profound potentials of a POSITIVE MENTAL ATTITUDE.

If you have your mental attitude under control you may control almost all other circumstances which affect your life, including your fears and worries of every nature whatsoever.

How Important Is Mental Attitude?

Let us analyze the part mental attitude plays in our lives and we shall learn how important it is.

Your mental attitude is the major factor which attracts people to you in a spirit of friendliness, or repels them, according to whether your attitude is positive or negative; and you are the only person who can determine which it shall be.

Mental attitude is an important factor in the maintenance of sound physical health. All doctors know, and most of them will admit, that the patient's mental attitude is more important in curing physical ailments than any other single factor.

Mental attitude is a determining factor—perhaps *the most important* factor—as to what results one gets from prayer. It has long been known that when one goes to prayer in a mental attitude swayed by fear, doubt, and anxiety, only negative results are experienced. Only the prayers which are backed by a mental attitude of profound FAITH can be expected to bring positive results.

Your mental attitude while driving an automobile on the public highway determines very largely whether you are a safe driver or a traffic hazard endangering your own life and the lives of others. Most automobile accidents are said to happen because of drunken driving, or anger, or some form of overanxiety or worry on the part of the drivers.

Your mental attitude determines, to a large extent, whether you find peace of mind or go through life in a state of frustration and misery.

Mental attitude is the warp and the woof of all salesmanship, regardless of what one is selling—merchandise, personal services, or any commodity. A person with a negative mental attitude can sell nothing. He may take an order from someone who buys something from him, but no *selling* was done. The transaction was entirely one of *buying*. Perhaps you have seen this truth demonstrated in many retail stores where the minds of the sales people clearly are not directed toward pleasing the customers.

Mental attitude controls, very largely, the space one occupies in life, the success one achieves, the friends one makes, and the contributions one makes to posterity. It would be no great overstatement of the truth if we said that mental attitude is EVERYTHING.

Mental attitude is the means by which one may condition his mind to go through surgery or dentistry without fear of physical pain. The means by which this can be accomplished are clearly described in subsequent chapters.

There are some who believe that one's mental attitude, while occupying the physical body during life, influences what happens to one after death. There is no positive proof of this theory except that it is obviously logical.

Lastly, the most convincing evidence of the importance of mental attitude is the fact that it is *the one and only thing* over which anyone has been given the complete, unchallengeable privilege of personal control. We cannot control the thoughts or the actions of other people. We cannot control either our coming into or going out of life, but we do have the inexorable privilege of controlling every thought we release from our minds, from the time we begin to think to the time that life is ended.

Here then is the most profound, the most significant of all facts which influence an individual's life! It is logical that by giving every person the complete control over his thinking the Creator intended this to be a priceless asset, and it is precisely that, because the mind is the one and only means by which an individual may plan his own life and live it as he chooses.

Henley, the poet, must have understood this great truth when he wrote the lines: "I am the Master of my Fate, I am the Captain of my Soul." Truly, we may become the captains of our worldly destiny precisely to the extent that we take possession of our minds and direct them to definite ends through control of our mental attitudes.

Mental Attitude Can Be Negative or Positive

Only a positive mental attitude pays off in the affairs of our everyday living, so let us see what it is, and how we may get it and apply it in the struggle for the things and circumstances we desire in life.

A positive mental attitude has many facets and innumerable combinations for its application in connection with every circumstance which affects our lives.

First of all, a positive mental attitude is the fixed purpose to make every experience, whether it is pleasant or unpleasant, yield some form of benefit which will help us to balance our lives with all the things which lead to peace of mind.

It is the habit of searching for "the seed of an equivalent benefit" which comes with every failure, defeat or adversity we experience, and causing that seed to germinate into something beneficial. Only a positive mental attitude can recognize and benefit by the lessons or the seed of an equivalent benefit which comes with all unpleasant things that one experiences.

A positive mental attitude is the habit of keeping the mind busily engaged in connection with the circumstances and things one desires in life, and *off* the things one does not desire. The majority of people go all the way through life with their mental attitudes dominated by fears and anxieties and worries over circumstances which somehow have a way of making their appearance sooner or later. And the strange part of this truth is that these people often blame other people for the misfortunes they have thus brought upon themselves by their negative mental attitudes.

The mind has a definite way of clothing one's thoughts in appropriate physical equivalents. Think in terms of poverty and you will live in poverty. Think in terms of opulence and you will attract opulence. *Through the eternal law of harmonious attraction one's thoughts always clothe themselves in material things appropriate unto their nature.*

A positive mental attitude is the habit of looking upon all unpleasant circumstances with which one meets as merely opportunities for one to test his capacity to rise above them by searching for that "seed of an equivalent benefit" and putting it to work.

A positive mental attitude is the habit of evaluating all problems, and distinguishing the difference between those one can master and those one cannot control. The person with a positive mental attitude endeavors to solve the problems he can control, and so relates himself to those he cannot control that they do not influence his mental attitude from positive to negative.

A positive mental attitude helps one to make allowances for the frailties and weaknesses of other people without becoming shocked by their negative-mindedness, or being influenced by their way of thinking.

A positive mental attitude is the habit of acting with definiteness of purpose, with full belief in both the soundness of that purpose and one's ability to achieve it.

It is the habit of going beyond the letter of one's responsibility and rendering more and better service than one is obligated to render, and doing it in a friendly, pleasing manner.

It is the habit of choosing a definite goal and marching forward toward its attainment without hesitating because of either commendation or condemnation.

It is the habit of looking for the good qualities in other people and expecting to find them, at the same time being prepared to recognize unfavorable qualities without being shocked into a negative state of mind.

It is the habit of mastering all the emotions by submitting them to examination by the head and the discipline of the power of will.

It is the habit of facing all the facts which affect one's life, both the pleasant and the unpleasant, and keeping a cool head when unpleasant emergencies arise.

It is recognition of the universal power of Infinite Intelligence, and the knowledge that it can be appropriated and directed to the attainment of definite ends through the medium of FAITH.

A positive mental attitude is the chief medium by which Alcoholics Anonymous has helped countless numbers of men and women to cure themselves of alcoholism. And it is also the basis of cure of the habit of excessive smoking.

It is the medium of all forms of "mind-conditioning" for whatsoever purposes, including the elimination of all types of fear.

All habits, good or bad, voluntary or involuntary, are established by one's mental attitude. It is the medium by which one may transmute unpleasant habits and circumstances into some form of benefit.

A positive mental attitude is the sole medium by which one may exercise the inherent right to maintain complete control over his own mind, without help or hindrance from anyone. And it is the means by which stumbling blocks may be transmuted into stepping stones of progress in every calling.

Mental attitude reveals itself from one person to another, without spoken words, signs or actions, by the medium of telepathy. Therefore, it is contagious.

A person's mental attitude while eating aids digestion or retards it, and a negative mental attitude can paralyze the digestive forces altogether.

The mental attitude of a public speaker often determines how his speech is interpreted, even more effectively than the words he uses. Again, the mental attitude of a writer while he is writing is conveyed to the reader, behind the lines of his writing.

By the proper conditioning and control of the mental attitude, one may condition his mind to meet any sort of unpleasant circumstance without becoming upset by it, including even the emergency of death of loved ones.

Mental attitude is a two-way gate across the pathway of life which can be swung one way into success and the other way into failure. The tragedy is that most people swing the gate in the wrong direction.

The patient's mental attitude is the doctor's best aid or his greatest hindrance in the treatment of physical ailments, depending upon whether the attitude is positive or negative.

From these statements of known facts one can easily understand why *mental attitude is everything,* because it influences every experience with which we meet, *and it is under our complete control at all times*.

What a profound thought it is to recognize that the one thing which can give us success or bring us failure, bless us with peace of mind, or curse us with misery all the days of our lives, is simply the privilege of taking possession of our own minds and guiding them to whatever ends we choose, through our mental attitude.

How Can One Control the Mental Attitude?

The starting point of control of the mental attitude is motive and desire. No one ever does anything without a motive, or motives, and the stronger the motive the easier it is to control the mental attitude.

Mental attitude can be influenced and controlled by a number of factors, such as:

(1) By a BURNING DESIRE for the attainment of a definite purpose based upon one or more of the nine basic motives which activate all human endeavor. (See the list of the nine basic motives in Chapter VII)

(2) By conditioning the mind to automatically choose and carry out definite positive objectives, with the aid of the EIGHT GUIDING PRINCES, or some similar technique which will keep the mind busily engaged with positive objectives, when one is asleep as well as when one is awake. (See description of the nature of the EIGHT GUIDING PRINCES in Chapter IV)

(3) By close association with people who inspire active engagement in positive purposes, and refusal to be influenced by negative-minded people.

(4) By auto-suggestion through which the mind is constantly given positive directives until it attracts only that for which these directives call.

(5) By a profound recognition, through its adoption and use, of the individual's exclusive privilege of controlling and directing his own mind.

(6) By the aid of a machine by which the subconscious mind can be given definite directives while one sleeps. (Such a machine is briefly described in Chapter IV)

Our great American Way of Life, our matchless system of free enterprise, and the personal liberty of which we feel so proud, are nothing more than the mental attitude of people organized and directed to specialized ends.

The one factor of the American Way of Life which stands out boldly above all others consists in the laws and the mechanisms of government we have set up to protect the individual in the freedom of control over his mental attitude.

It was this freedom of control over mental attitude which gave us the great leaders who patterned our American Way of Life and our great system of free enterprise. *And it is significant that only those who moved with a positive mental attitude became leaders.*

Thomas A. Edison's positive mental attitude sustained him through more than ten thousand failures and led him to the discovery of the incandescent electric light which ushered in the great electrical age and the fabulous riches it gave us.

Henry Ford's positive mental attitude kept him afloat during his early struggles in building his first automobile, and it served as his greatest and most important asset in establishing the monumental industrial empire which made him richer than Croesus and provided employment, directly and indirectly, for perhaps more than ten million men and women.

Andrew Carnegie's positive mental attitude lifted him up from poverty and obscurity and served as his major asset in the establishment of an industry which gave birth to the great steel age, which now serves as the most important link in our entire economic system.

Mahatma Gandhi's positive mental attitude (he called it passive resistance) was more than a match for the great power of the British military forces which ruled India for many generations. It was Gandhi's positive mental attitude which brought together a Master Mind alliance of more than two hundred million of his fellowmen who gave mighty power to his "passive resistance" and freed India from British control without the firing of a gun or the loss of a single soldier.

It was the positive mental attitude of the builder of the magnificent Golden Gate suspension bridge which gave us the world's longest single-span bridge, despite the fact that his first attempt indicated that the job was an engineering impossibility.

Wherever we find leadership and great achievement at any level of life, in any calling or occupation, we recognize that it is founded upon a positive mental attitude.

A positive mental attitude is the sum total of hopes, wishes, and beliefs, added up and transmuted into FAITH! And Faith is the open door to Infinite Intelligence which can be appropriated and used *only by those who maintain a positive mental attitude*.

And the most profound fact regarding a positive mental attitude is that everyone has the privilege of adopting it and using it for all purposes, *without money and without price*.

The secret by which this profound truth may enrich your mind, and give you mastery over obstacles to happiness which you may encounter the remainder of your life, has been revealed in the chapters which follow.

Read with an open mind and you will be rewarded with a form of riches sufficient to give you a well-balanced life, freedom from fear, and peace of mind which shall endure. In the chapters which follow you will be introduced to the greatest person now living. When you discover the name of this person, mark the page where the name was revealed, and sign it, for you will have discovered a new meaning of the purpose for which we are on this planet for the brief span of years called Life.

In the chapters which follow, minute instructions have been presented for adjusting the mental attitude to eliminate the fear of dental or medical surgery. This chapter on mental attitude is a sort of preview which will prepare you to accept and use those instructions for the elimination of unpleasantness in connection with surgery or any other undesirable circumstances with which you may meet.

CHAPTER II

A Visit through the Valley of Life's Miracles

A little while ago I turned back the pages of the Great Book of Time in which my own magnificent interlude with Life has been recorded, and on the pages marked, "Things I Have Discarded as Being Either Harmless or Useless in Life," I discovered a gold mine of riches which I shall reveal through this volume.

Why did I wait so long to make this discovery of the fabulous riches I had overlooked? The answer will be obvious when the nature of my discovery has been described. Before I could make this discovery I had to come of age spiritually; I had to trade youth for maturity in order to gain sufficient wisdom to give me the capacity to recognize, and properly interpret, these great riches "from within" through eyes which are not deceived by the false habits of men.

As I slowly turned the pages of this astounding record in the Book of Time, I was shocked to discover that everything, every circumstance known to man, every mistake and every failure and every heartache, may become highly beneficial when one relates himself to them in a spirit of harmony and understanding of their nature and purpose.

And I was agreeably surprised to learn, by analyzing all the circumstances of my past which I had considered unpleasant and harmful at the time, *that each of these had yielded many of the only things of permanent value which I now possess.*

During my exploration of this Great Book of Time, I discovered a previously unknown method by which all of man's past failures, mistakes, and frustrations may be transmuted into the richest blessings known to mankind. It was this discovery which left me no alternative but to write this volume for the benefit of those who are groping in darkness for the way to peace of mind, just as I was blindly searching for it for nearly forty years.

Before I rummaged through the scrap heap of ideas and things I had feared and discarded as useless, I believed the secret of successful achievement could be revealed only by studying those who were successful.

Having been commissioned by Andrew Carnegie to give the world its first practical philosophy of success, and through Mr. Carnegie, having had close access to more than five hundred of the top-ranking successes of his era, I naturally looked to these men of great achievement as the only source of usable knowledge worthy of consideration by those who are trying to find their places in an intensively competitive world.

I have now abandoned this false conclusion, for I have discovered that the eternal laws of successful human achievement are as available to the poor and the humble as they are to the rich and the proud.

My first shocking realization of this great truth came with my first meeting with an uneducated black man who was born in the South and earned his bread by the sweat of his brow. When I first heard of his story, I sought him out and gave him a searching and critical analysis, for I had a keen desire to learn the true secret of his dramatic rebirth from rags to riches within an unbelievably brief time.

On a hot summer day this man stopped at the end of a row of cotton, leaned on his hoe handle, mopped his brow, and cried out in agony: *"Oh, Lord! why do I have to work like this and get nothing out of it but a hut to sleep in and sow-belly to eat?"*

His cry brought an answer and started a series of events which changed the lives of millions of people who were destined to hear his story.

I have chosen this man's story as an introduction to this chapter, because it so perfectly illustrates the soundness of the counsel I shall offer through subsequent chapters to those who are searching for material riches, peace of mind, and a better understanding of the means of mastering all unpleasant circumstances.

Because of the place of his birth and the color of his skin, this man had two strikes against him from the start, *but purely by that chance question,* he tuned in on one of the great miracles of life, which will be described later, and lifted himself to a position of fame and fortune unknown to the majority of people—even those who have had the privilege of formal educations in our great universities.

First of all, the answer to the man's question gave him contact with the first principle of personal success, *Definiteness of Purpose,* and a definite plan for its attainment. And that purpose was nothing less than the trading of his old personality for a much greater one—a personality *with the power to acquire whatever it desired regardless of race, creed, or color*—the sort of personality I shall endeavor to help every reader of this volume to attain.

Forthwith, in compliance with the answer the man received to his question, he appointed himself to the high Priesthood as God In Person, the one and only true living

God to all the people of the earth. Whatever one may think of the man's choice of a Definite Major Purpose, he cannot be charged with an inferiority complex, which is the dominating influence in so many lives.

Now, before any conclusions are reached concerning this man's self-appointment to so high a station in life, let me give a briefing as to how far he has already gone in the attainment of his Major Purpose. Perhaps you will sober your judgment of him, and instead of condemning him, it might be more beneficial if you found out something of the powers he adopted to raise himself to his ultimate high position in life.

This man gave himself the very impressive pseudonym of Father Divine. He gained a following estimated as in the millions, including large numbers of whites, located in nearly every state of the U.S. and in some foreign countries.

Father Divine was given the stewardship of vast amounts of money, all in the form of voluntary donations. He traveled in a RollsRoyce and slept in his own hotels in many of the cities where he visited, so there was never a question of his staying in any but the pleasantest accommodations; the color bar did not affect him. His huge and complex organization operated many kinds of businesses, from pushcarts to dress shops and restaurants—all staffed by volunteer help.

How much good Father Divine's opulence brought to others is of no concern here. I do not mean to sell Father Divine to anyone at this late date, certainly.

However, it is the author's purpose to acquaint you with the nature of the "miracle" that Father Divine stumbled upon, perhaps by sheer chance, which gave him fredom from the handicap of his race and color, as well as freedom from the handicap of poverty and lack of education, and made him exceedingly rich.

This information is intended for your benefit, not that you may emulate Father Divine, but to inspire you to excel him in your own chosen field of service to mankind, whether it be in the realm of religion or in some other useful service. Or you may be content to use the information merely for softening the burdens of your own personal life.

The secret of Father Divine's riches is not new to me. I have devoted over forty years to its study, and I have seen it work successfully in the lives of more than five hundred of the outstanding men of this nation with whom I have worked, and who collaborated with me over a long period of years in the organization of the Science of Success—men like Henry Ford, Thomas A. Edison, Dr. Alexander Graham Bell, Woodrow Wilson, and William Howard Taft.

The strangest fact concerning this supreme secret of personal success, as revealed by close study of those distinguished men with whom I worked, was that not one of them—with the exception of three—understood the real source of their success, or the nature of the power which made it possible on so fabulous a scale. The vast majority of them stumbled upon this great "miracle" very much in the same manner as did Father Divine.

Those who are seeking the true secret of his achievements will not overlook the fact that if he had a voluntary following of thirty million people, or even one million, he must have possessed some mysterious power of attraction not usually possessed by those who are motivated entirely by greed for material things.

Here, as in other chapters, the author has endeavored to emphasize the fact that the secret of financial prosperity is precisely the same as that through which one may transmute physical pain or any unpleasant circumstance into benefits.

In this chapter, and in those which follow, I shall fully describe the "miracle" responsible for Father Divine's success, but I shall do more than that. I shall describe some additional miracles available to all the people of the earth—miracles which are only partially recognized and seldom used, although they provide the real path to peace of mind and material riches in abundance.

All, except approximately one person out of every ten million people who may read the list of "miracles" I shall describe, will be shocked and surprised to learn that I have listed them as potential riches of the highest order. That one person out of every ten million will not be shocked or surprised because he or she will belong in the same class with the Edisons, and the Fords, and the Father Divines who stumbled upon the "miracle" and used it to shape destiny to their own self-styled patterns of life.

As we travel through the "Valley of Life's Miracles," one of which was definitely responsible for Father Divine's transition from extreme poverty and ignorance into fabulous wealth, and wisdom sufficient to manage it, you will have reason to rejoice if you recognize the particular "miracle" by which this change was wrought. If you do not make the discovery in this chapter, it may be revealed to you in subsequent chapters, where I have recorded all that is known of the path that leads to peace of mind and plenty.

Here are some cues which may aid you in analyzing Father Divine accurately:

The exact time, place, and circumstances where his new birth took place were matters entirely of his own choice *and under his control.*

No one aided him or suggested to him the possibility of his throwing off ignorance and poverty, and taking on in their place fabulous wealth and wisdom. This point is emphasized because naturally it suggests that *whatever an uneducated man has done, any other person of equal mental capacity may duplicate or excel,* in any chosen field of human endeavor.

Could anyone reasonably doubt that the formula, through which this man exchanged poverty for vast riches, may also serve to transmute any undesirable circumstance into a benefit of equivalent proportions?

Wherein does the difference exist between this particular man and the others of his race who live in the United States, and who have the same privileges he had acquired for himself? The answer to this question may give you a sound clue to the "miracle" which transformed this self-appointed Messiah from a nobody, in the direst of poverty, to a somebody, in command of overabundance.

The "miracle" responsible for Father Divine's changed life is precisely the same as that which lifted Henry Ford and Thomas A. Edison and Andrew Carnegie to stupendous heights of personal achievement in their respective fields, and it is the same "miracle" which has been responsible for all of the progress made by the human race in all fields of endeavor.

Through the aid of this "miracle," Milo C. Jones, owner of a small farm near Fort Atkinson, Wisconsin, made himself a millionaire after he had been stricken with double paralysis; and he found his success *on the same farm* where previously he had made only a fair living.

Students of the author who have found prosperity, solved "impossible" personal problems, and found peace of mind through the aid of the "miracle," are legion. They exist in nearly every walk of life, every business, every profession, throughout a large portion of the world. For this reason the illustrations given throughout this volume have been adequately authenticated over more than forty years of research.

Dr. Frank Crane was the pastor of a small church in Chicago, from which he barely earned a living. As a student of this author he discovered the "miracle" that yielded him the idea of publishing his sermons in a syndicated newspaper column which brought him an income of more than $75,000 yearly.

What has all this to do with the mastery of fear and physical pain and sorrow, and the multiple frustrations one may encounter throughout life? Just how can the principle which helps people become financially rich serve as well to separate physical pain from the dentist's drill or the surgeon's scalpel?

Be patient, read carefully, with an open mind, and you shall have the answers to these and all other questions which may arise in your mind before the "miracle" is revealed to you.

If you should impatiently demand that the "miracle" be revealed in the first chapter of this volume, the author would answer by telling you of something which happened while he was a very small boy, but which made a lasting impression on his mind.

Grandfather took some corn out to the chicken house, scattered it over the dirt floor and then carefully covered it with straw. When asked why he went to all this trouble, he replied, "For two very good reasons: Number one, covering the corn with straw so the chickens will have to scratch to find it, gives them the exercise they need to be healthy; and secondly, it gives them a chance to get pleasure from showing how smart they are in finding the corn which they think I tried to hide from them."

And now let us turn to the analysis of some of the minor "miracles" one must understand and properly evaluate before the nature of the major "miracle," which gives one a transformed life, can be revealed. Perhaps the most misunderstood of all these "miracles" is the one described in the next chapter, because it reveals the starting place from which one must take off in exchanging the circumstances of life he does not desire for those which he covets.

CHAPTER III

The Law of Growth through Change
The First Miracle of Life

ETERNAL CHANGE has been chosen to head the list of the Miracles of Life, not essentially because it is the most important of those here described, but for the reason that it is the one *most bitterly opposed* by the vast majority of the human race. Failure to understand it and adapt oneself to it is the major cause of all personal failures and defeats.

The changes in our way of living have revealed, during the first half of the twentieth century, more of nature's secrets than had been uncovered during the entire past of civilization. Among these have been the invention of the automobile, the telephone, radio, television, talking pictures, airplanes, radar, and wireless telegraphy—all produced by everchanging processes of the human mind.

Change is the tool of human progress, in the affairs of nations not less than in the lives of individuals. And the business or industry which neglects to keep moving forward through change is doomed to failure.

The great American way of life, which has provided the people with the highest standard of living the world has ever known, has been the product of continuous change.

The Law of Change is one of Nature's inexorable laws, without which there could have been no such reality as civilization. Without the law of change the human race would still be where it started from—on the plane with all the other animals and creatures of the earth which are eternally bound and limited by a pattern of instinct, beyond which they never can rise.

Through the law of change (popularly known as evolution), the human race has slowly left the baseline of the animal family, where the destiny of all living things was fixed by a life pattern of instinct, and has evolved into higher and still higher degrees of intelligence, until man now is something infinitely greater than the thirty-thousand man-made gods whom he has created and worshiped since the beginning of his long and tortuous trip upward.

The entire history of mankind, the record of life in all its forms, is a clearly marked pattern of perpetual change. No living thing is the same two minutes in succession, and this change is so inexorable that the entire physical body of man undergoes a complete change, and a replacement of all the physical cells of the body, every seven months.

The law of change is the Creator's device for separating man from the remainder of the animal families. It is also the device by which the eternal verities of life, the habits and the thoughts of men, are continuously reshaping themselves into a better system of human relations leading toward harmony and better understanding among men. And it is one of the devices one must use in mastering fixed habits which cause the fear of physical pain.

Through the law of change, the habits of men, which do not conform to the overall pattern and purpose of the universe, are periodically broken up by wars, epidemics of disease, drouth, and other irresistible forces of nature which force man to free himself from the effects of his follies and start all over again. This same law of change, which levels the peoples of all nations to the baseline of the overall plan of the universe, *applies with equal force to individuals who fail to interpret and adapt themselves to nature's laws.*

"Conform to the overall plan or perish," is nature's warning!

The fears and the failures of men, the shocks and disappointments in human relations, all are designed to shake man loose from habits to which he so tenaciously clings, *so he may adopt, embrace, and benefit by better habits of growth.*

The whole purpose of education, or so it should be at least, is to start the mind of the individual to growing and developing *from within;* to cause the mind to evolve and expand through constant changes in the thinking processes, so that the individual may eventually become acquainted with his own potential powers and thereby be capable of solving his personal problems.

Evidence that this theory conforms with nature's plans may be found in the fact that the better educated people of all times are those who graduate from the great UNIVERSITY OF HARD KNOCKS, through experiences *which force them to develop and use their mind-power.*

The law of change is one of the greatest of all sources of education! Understand this truth and you will no longer oppose the changes which give you a wider scope of understanding of yourself and of the world at large. And you will no longer resist nature's breaking up of some of the habits you have formed *which have not brought you peace of mind or material riches.*

The traits the Creator most emphatically frowns upon in human beings are complacency, self-satisfaction, procrastination, fear and self-imposed limitations, all of which carry heavy penalties which are exacted from those who indulge such traits.

Through the law of change, man is forced to keep on growing. Whenever a nation, a business institution, or an individual, ceases to change and settles into a rut of routine habits, some mysterious power enters and smashes the setup, breaks up the old habits, lays the foundation for new and better habits.

In everything and everyone the law of growth is through eternal change!

Flexibility of personality—the capacity of an individual to adapt himself to all the circumstances which affect his life—is one of the major factors of an attractive personality. Also it is the medium of adaptability to the great law of growth through change.

The Ford Motor Company was pyramided from the humble beginning of a one-room brick factory into one of the world's greatest industrial empires, which provides directly and indirectly employment for hundreds of thousands of people.

Henry Ford, the founder, despite all his traits of genius in industrial management, very nearly wrecked the business on at least two occasions because his capacity for flexibility—the ability to change—had not kept up with his years. After his death the business was taken over by his grandson, a mere youth in comparison with the founder of the business, but a young man with great flexibility and willingness to follow the law of growth through change. In a matter of a few years the young man transformed the Ford industrial empire into an institution far in advance of anything his grandfather had accomplished during his entire lifetime.

In labor relations, in industrial management, in automobile designing and styling, young Henry Ford proved himself to be a man who invited change instead of fighting it, and by this application of wisdom, made of himself an industrial wizard overnight.

On every hand the soul of man cries out, saying in effect: Wake up, get wise to yourself, throw off your old habits before they bind you in slavery and force you to come back for another try at life through a new incarnation. If you wish to finish the job while you are here, you must adapt yourself to the great law of change and continue to grow.

The soul of man cries out in words of warning and says: Everything, every circumstance which touches your life, whether it be pleasant or unpleasant, is grist for your Mill of Life. Embrace it as such, grind it into your chosen pattern of living and let it serve instead of tormenting you through fear and worry.

An old Virginia family was born and reared in the mountains of southwest Virginia, in comparative poverty. At long last the railroads came and the rich coal fields were put into operation. This family sold their mountain land for a fabulous sum, moved into town, and built a new modern home. When the house was completed, with three bathrooms equipped with all modern conveniences, the wife refused to permit the contractor to be paid because she claimed the job had not been finished.

"What," the contractor inquired, "is missing?"

"You know well enough what is missing," the wife replied. "There is no backhouse on the place."

"Well," explained the surprised contractor, "backhouses went out of style when you moved to town. You now have three beautiful bathrooms where you may perform all necessary bodily attentions in private and with great comfort."

"All my life," the wife exclaimed, "I have enjoyed reading Sears and Roebuck's catalogue in my backhouse, and I have no intention of giving up that pleasure at my age. Build that backhouse or you'll get no money."

The backhouse was built! When the wife inspected it she argued, "It will not do! It has only one hole in the seat and we have always had two holes."

So another hole was provided, and for good measure the contractor installed plumbing for hot and cold water, also a telephone, so the wealthy old lady could attend to her social duties and read her Sears and Roebuck catalogue in the backhouse.

Complacency and old habits had won a victory over change and progress.

When cash registers were first introduced, the manufacturers had great difficulty in getting merchants to install them, and sales people in general went into spasms over them. Store clerks frowned upon the new devices as being a suggestion that they were dishonest, and merchants protested that the cost of the machines, plus the time required for their operation, would eat too deeply into their profits.

But the law of change is persistent and inevitable! Today no merchant in his right mind would try to operate a retail business, in which anyone but himself had to handle cash receipts, without the aid of the cash register.

When the Federal Reserve Banking System was forced into operation by the Congress of the United States, the bankers in general sent up a howl of protest. The system meant radical change, and the bankers, like everyone else, were opposed to any changes which broke up their established ways of doing business. The Federal Reserve Banking System proved to be the greatest safeguard for the banks that was ever introduced, and today if it were suggested that the system be abolished, the bankers probably would put up an equally loud cry against the change.

Of the utmost significance is the fact that the Creator provided man with the one and only means by which he has broken away from the animal family and ascended into spiritual estates, where he may be the master of his own earthly fate. The means thus provided is the law of change. By the simple process of changing his mental attitude, man can draw for himself any pattern of life and living he chooses and make that pattern a reality. This is the one and only thing over which man has been provided with irrevocable, unchallenged, and unchallengeable powers of absolute control—a fact which suggests that it must have been considered by the Creator to be the most important prerogative of man.

Dictators and would-be world conquerors come and they

go. They always *go* because it is not a part of the overall plan of the universe for man to be enslaved. It is rather a part of the eternal pattern that every man shall be free, to live his own life his own way, to control his thoughts and his deeds, to make his own earthly destiny.

That is why the philosopher, who looks backward into the past to determine what is going to happen in the yet unborn future, cannot get excited because a Hitler or a Stalin momentarily basks in the light of his own ego and threatens the freedom of mankind. For these men, like all others of their ilk who have preceded them, will destroy themselves with their own excesses and vanities and their lusts for power over the free world. Moreover, these would-be stranglers of human freedom may be only demons who unwittingly serve as shock troops to awaken man from his complacency and make way for the change that will bring new and better ways of living.

Nature leads man through change after change by peaceful means as long as man cooperates, but she resorts to revolutionary methods if man rebels and neglects or refuses to conform to the law of change. The revolutionary method may consist in the death of a loved one or a severe illness; it may bring a failure in business, or the loss of a job, which forces the individual to change his occupation and seek employment in an entirely new field, where he will find greater opportunities which he would never have known if his old habits had not been broken up.

Nature enforces the law of fixation of habits in every living thing lower than man, and just as definitely enforces the law of change in the habits of man. Nature thus provides the only means by which man may grow and evolve in accordance with his fixed position in the overall plan of the universe.

Thomas A. Edison's first major adversity was experienced when his teacher sent him home after only three months in a graded school, with a note to his parents saying he did not have the capacity to take an education.

He never went back to school—a conventional school, that is—but he began to school himself in the great University of Hard Knocks, where he gained an education which made him one of the greatest inventors of all times. Before he was graduated from that university he was fired from one job after another, while the hand of Destiny guided him through the *essential changes* which prepared him to become a great inventor. A formal schooling perhaps would have spoiled his chances of becoming great.

Nature knows what she is about when adversity, physical pain, sorrow, distress, failure and temporary defeat overtake one. Remember this and profit by it the next time you meet with adversity. And instead of crying out in rebellion, or shivering with fear, hold your head high and look in all directions for that seed of an equivalent benefit which is carried in every circumstance of adversity.

I am never frightened by revolutionary changes in my life, whether they are voluntary, or forced upon me by circumstances of an unpleasant nature over which I have no control, *for I do at least have control over my reaction to these circumstances*. And I exercise this privilege, not by complaining, but by searching for that seed of an equivalent benefit which each experience carries with it.

The book you are reading is literally the product of over forty years of continuous and oftentimes drastic changes I have had to make in my way of life. Many of the changes were forced; some of them were voluntary, but all of them added up, at long last, to the revelation of the secret of peace of mind and material prosperity.

When I was commissioned by Andrew Carnegie to begin research in preparation for the organization of the world's first practical philosophy of personal achievement, I was so little prepared for the job that truthfully I did not know the meaning of the word "philosophy" until I looked it up in a dictionary.

If ever anyone began a job by starting at scratch, I began right there! What I had to do to prepare myself for the successful fulfillment of the assignment Mr. Carnegie had given me was not mere change; it was practically a *complete rebuilding job!* Perhaps this was fortunate because the knowledge I gained from my own personal struggles led eventually to the revelation of the supreme "miracle" which is the central purpose in writing this volume.

The rebuilding job included the changing of self-made habits of failure for self-made habits of success, which at long last gave me a balanced life that includes everything I desire or need for the style of living I have chosen.

Among other changes I had to make in preparation for my life work were these:

(a) Curing of the habit of selling myself short because of lack of self-confidence.

(b) Freeing myself from the habit of yielding to the seven basic fears, including the fear of ill health and physical pain.

(c) Removing the habit of binding myself to penury and want through my self-imposed limitations.

(d) Breaking the habit of neglect in taking possession of my own mind and directing it to the attainment of all my desires.

(e) Curing myself of the habit of failure to relate myself to recognition and freedom from want in a spirit of humble gratitude.

(f) Changing the habit of expecting to reap before I had sown. (Confusing my NEEDS with my RIGHTS to receive.)

(g) Curing myself of the false belief that HONESTY and SINCERITY OF PURPOSE alone will lead to success.

(h) Changing the false belief that EDUCATION comes only through the media of higher learning.

(i) Correcting the habit of neglecting to schedule my life on a practical budget and use of TIME.

- (j) Curing myself of the habit of failure to devote the major portion of my TIME to the pursuit of my Definite Major Purpose in life.
- (k) Changing my habit of impatience.
- (l) Correcting the habit of failure to take inventory of all my intangible riches and express gratitude for them.
- (m) Correction of the habit of endeavoring to accumulate more material riches than I could legitimately use.
- (n) Correcting the habit of believing it is more beneficial to RECEIVE than to GIVE.
- (o) Last, but not least, correcting the habit of neglect in recognizing the source of Infinite Intelligence and the means of contacting and using it for any desired purpose—by application of the SUPREME MIRACLE.

These do not represent the entire list of changes I had to make in my habits of thought and action, but they are some of the more important ones, from which it will be obvious that the LAW OF CHANGE has played an important part of my life, and just as obvious, that had I not made these changes, I would have deprived myself of the privilege of giving the world a workable philosophy of personal success, which has brought me more recognition than one person needs on this plane of life.

In presenting these intimate circumstances of my life so frankly, I hope you will recognize that I am preparing you to accept the truth that perhaps you too will need to change some of your habits before you may enjoy a full, well-balanced life made to your own pattern and style of living.

The extent to which you will need to make changes in your present habits is entirely something you will have to decide, but the list must include the mastery of the seven basic fears if you aspire to the attainment of a well-balanced life, which includes peace of mind.

The seven basic fears are as follows:

(1) The Fear of POVERTY
(2) The Fear of CRITICISM
(3) The Fear of ILL HEALTH and PHYSICAL PAIN
(4) The Fear of the LOSS of LOVE
(5) The Fear of the LOSS of LIBERTY
(6) The Fear of OLD AGE
(7) The Fear of DEATH

In the chapters which follow you will be given instructions for the mastery of these and all other fears, through the application of new habits of thinking which you must develop and use in the place of the old habits which have made these fears possible. Whatever other changes may be necessary to give you a well-rounded life will not alter the fact that mastery of these seven basic fears is a "must" in your rebuilding program.

Take heart from the promise that these corrective instructions will impose upon you no hardships nor actions beyond your ability to control. They have a price attached to them, but it is a price well within the means of all normal people.

We are where we are and what we are because of our daily habits!

Our habits are under our individual control and they may be changed at any time by the mere will to change them. This prerogative is the one and only privilege over which the individual has complete control. Habits are made by our thinking, and our thinking is the one thing over which the Creator gave us complete right of control; and along with this right profound rewards for our exercising the right, and terrible penalties for our failure to exercise it.

CHAPTER IV

Our Unseen Guides
The Second Miracle of Life

OUR UNSEEN GUIDES, whose existence can be proved only by those who have recognized them and accepted their services, remain at our service from the time of our birth until our death.

These invisible talismans remain with us while we are awake and watch over us while we sleep, although most people go through life without recognizing their existence.

It is not my purpose to give a long dissertation as evidence of the existence of unseen guides who aid human beings, but merely to bring them to the attention of my fellow wayfarers who are willing to accept whatever sources of aid they can find in their search for a way of life which satisfies one's needs and leads to peace of mind.

Had it not been for the aid I received from my friendly unseen guides, I never could have given the world the Science of Success which now aids millions of people to recognize and make practical use of their *inner sources of power*.

Eight of my unseen guides have been recognized and

named, each with a name appropriate to the nature of the service it renders. They are here described in detail, but one should keep in mind the fact that the Eight Guiding Princes are the product of my own imagination and they may be duplicated by anyone who chooses to engage them.

I treat my Eight Guiding Princes as though they were real people whose entire services are at my command throughout life. I give them orders and thank them for their services just as I would do if they were people. And they react to my requests as though they were real people.

A description of the Eight Guiding Princes, together with an explanation of the service each performs, now follows.

The Eight Guiding Princes

1. PRINCE OF FINANCIAL PROSPERITY

The sole responsibility of this invisible guide is to keep me adequately supplied with every material thing which I desire or need to maintain the style of living which I have adopted. Money worries, which destroy the peace of mind of so many people throughout their lives, are something I never experience. When I need money it is always available in whatever amounts I may require, *but money is neither expected nor obtained without my giving something of equal value in return*—usually in some form of service rendered for the benefit of others.

2. PRINCE OF SOUND PHYSICAL HEALTH

The sole responsibility of this invisible guide is that of keeping my physical body in perfect order at all times, including the conditioning of the body for any adjustments which have to be made, such as that of preparation for dentistry. Before this Prince took over I was subject to headaches, constipation, and at times physical exhaustion, all of which have been corrected. The Prince of Sound Physical Health keeps all the vital organs of my body alert and functioning at all times, keeps the billions of individual cells of my body properly charged with bodily resistance, *and provides adequate immunity against all contagious diseases.*

Let it be remembered, however, that I cooperate with the Prince of Sound Physical Health by sensible living habits, such as proper eating, the right amount of sleep, *and habits which balance my work with an equal amount of play.* But particularly, *I keep my mind occupied with positive, constructive thinking,* and never permit it to engage in any form of fear, superstition or hypochondria. And lastly, with every morsel of food and every drop of liquid which goes into my mouth *I add a generous mixture of worship,* through which I express thanks to my invisible guide, the Prince of Sound Physical Health, for maintenance of perfect health throughout my body.

I enjoy a peaceful calmness throughout my life, in all of my activities and experiences, but especially do I make it a business to eat my food in an atmosphere of joyous serenity. We have no set hour for family discipline in our home, but if we did have such an hour *it would not be at meal time,* as is the case in many homes.

Every thought one expresses while eating becomes a part of the energy which goes into the food and enters the blood stream, and that thought makes its way to the brain where it blesses or curses one according to whether the thought is positive or negative. Evidence of this truth may be found in the case of the mother who nurses her child at her breast. If she becomes worried or negative-minded for any reason while the child is nursing, her state of mind will poison her milk and give the child indigestion or cholic. And of course it is well known to doctors that most stomach ulcers are due mainly to worry and negative thinking.

It is obvious, therefore, that the Prince of Sound Physical Health must have a considerable amount of intelligent cooperation in order to keep the physical body operating efficiently and normally. This is the price one must pay for good health.

3. PRINCE OF PEACE OF MIND

The sole responsibility of this invisible guide is to keep the mind free from disturbing influences, such as fear, superstition, greed, envy, hatred and covetousness. The work of the Prince of Peace of Mind is closely related to that of the Prince of Sound Physical Health. Through the work of this invisible guide, one may shut off all thoughts of unpleasant circumstances of the past and all thoughts of unpleasant experiences contemplated for the future, such as that of surgical operations or dentistry.

The Prince of Peace of Mind keeps the mind so fully occupied with subjects of one's choosing that there is no space left in it for voluntary, stray thoughts of a negative nature. *To these, the doors of the mind are tightly closed!* This invisible guide throws a wall of protection around one, which keeps out everything which could lead to worry or fear or anxiety of any nature, except only those circumstances which have a legitimate right to consideration in connection with one's obligations to others; and these are so modified that they are easily managed.

There always are human relations which may be unpleasant temporarily, which one must recognize and deal with—such as the details of management of a business, or a profession or job, or the family budget—and there always are unpleasant emergencies one must meet—such as the death of friends or loved ones. To all of these the Prince of Peace of Mind helps the individual relate himself *without being thrown off mental balance.*

4. PRINCE OF HOPE ⎫
5. PRINCE OF FAITH ⎬ Operating as twins.
⎭

The sole responsibility of these invisible guides is that of keeping the gateway to Infinite Intelligence open to me at all times, under all circumstances. These twins keep me from handicapping myself with unnecessary limitations in connection with my life work, and they help me to so organize my plans that *they conform to the laws of nature and the rights of my fellowmen.* They help me also to see my plans a completed reality, *even before I begin putting them into operation;* and they turn me back from undertaking any plan or purpose which, if it were carried out, might be of ultimate harm to me or to others.

The Princes of Hope and Faith keep me in constant touch with the spiritual forces which operate through me, and they guide me toward objectives which benefit everyone with whom I come into contact, either in person or by my written works. There then is the explanation as to why the readers of my books are so universally successful in the planning and the living of their own lives.

These Princes of Hope and Faith keep me charged with enthusiasm sufficient to insure me against procrastination. They keep my imagination alert and active in planning the work to which I devote my entire life. They help me find joy and happiness in everything I do. And they help me interpret the evils of the world without embracing them or being injured by them. They help me walk with all men, both the saints and the sinners, *and still remain the master of my own fate, the captain of my own soul!* They keep my ego alert and active, yet humble and grateful. And lastly, they help me ride the waves of chaos and confusion in a world which is undergoing rapid changes in human relations, *without giving up or neglecting my own inalienable privilege of controlling and directing my own mind to whatsoever ends I may choose.*

With Hope and Faith as my constant guides I meet successfully the resistances and the unpleasant experiences of life by transmuting them into positive forces, through which I carry my aims and purposes to conclusion. With the aid of these twin guides everything which comes to my mill of life is made into the grist of opportunity.

6. PRINCE OF LOVE   ⎫ Operating as twins
7. PRINCE OF ROMANCE ⎬

The sole responsibility of these invisible guides is to

keep me youthful in both body and mind, and they do their work so well that I celebrate every birthday *by deducting a year from my age!* And the joyful result is that I feel, think, work, and play as if I were twenty years younger.

The Princes of Love and Romance make of my work a joy which knows not discouragement or fatigue, *and they stimulate my imagination to create with ease the patterns of all things I desire to accomplish.*

These invisible guides help me to live again the loves and the fantasies of the days which have flown, and they bring back memories of past experiences which have served to introduce me to my "other self;" that self which embraces the beauties and avoids the unpleasantness of life.

Love and Romance have aided me in exchanging for wisdom the sorrows, frustrations and failures of the past, and they have given refinement to my soul which could have been attained by no other means. They help me recognize the objective of my earthly destiny and provide me with the means of surmounting the obstacles I must surmount to attain my destiny. They help me in making every day of my life pay off in dividends of joy which more than compensate for the necessity of struggle that each day calls for.

Love and Romance have made me flexible and adaptable to all the circumstances which affect my life, both the pleasant and the unpleasant, so that I do not forfeit the privilege of controlling and directing my mind to whatsoever ends I choose.

They provide me with a keen sense of humanity with which I adjust myself favorably in all my human relations, and they help me attract the people and the circumstances which I need to make me grateful for my sojourn in life.

Love and Romance help me recognize and germinate and develop in growth that seed of an equivalent benefit which comes in every adversity, every frustration, every failure and every disappointment.

Love and Romance are the sole means by which I gracefully exchange youth for the wisdom with which I write my own price tag on the business of living *and make Life pay off on my own terms.* And they restrain me from *wanting too much;* prevent me from *settling for too little.* They have taught me to pray, "Help me, O Lord, to acquire the things which are good for me and prevent me from acquiring things I do not need."

Love and Romance are the interior decorators of the upper room in which dwells my soul! They make me grateful for the things I have; keep me from sorrowing over the things I have not. And should I indulge my Love where it is not reciprocated, Romance helps me find compensation in the joy I had *in the indulgence itself,* and recognize that Love rebounds to the benefit of those who express it, even though it may not be reciprocated.

Love and Romance help me express pity for others where, without these guides, I might express hatred, and they heal quickly the wounds inflicted upon me by the injuries and injustices of others.

8. PRINCE OF OVERALL WISDOM

The responsibilities of this Prince consist in multiple services. First of all, the Prince of Overall Wisdom inspires eternal action on the part of the other seven Princes to the end that each carries out his duties to the fullest extent possible, and protects me while I sleep the same as while I am awake.

This invisible guide performs another, and a very miraculous service, by transmuting into benefits to me *all the failures and defeats and unpleasant circumstances I have experienced in the past,* so that everything which has affected my life in the past has been converted into an asset of great value.

The Prince of Overall Wisdom gives me guidance at the crossroads of life, whenever I may be in doubt as to which road to take, and gives me the go-ahead or a stop signal in connection with all my aims, plans and purposes.

There are other unseen Guides at my service whose names I do not know. Nor do I understand completely the full extent and nature of the services they render, except that whatever I may need to carry on my life work, or whatever I may desire *to give me continuous peace of mind,* is always at my command without effort or anxiety on my part.

These mysterious Guides first came to my attention many years ago, by interrupting my plans with definite failure when I strayed away from my major mission in life—that mission being the organization and the spreading of the Science of Success. From time to time, as I gained recognition from the public in connection with my life work, I was offered what seemed to me fabulous opportunities to commercialize my talents and my experience. One of these opportunities was offered me by the late Ivy Lee, Public Relations Counsellor for the Rockefeller family. Although the deal never was consummated, I did accept the offer, and that mere acceptance cost me the loss of the *Golden Rule Magazine* which I had founded as a by-product of my philosophy.

After I had met with one failure after another, and each time was tempted to desert or neglect my major mission in life, I began to notice that the effects of each failure were immediately wiped out the moment I got back on the track and began to carry out my mission. This happened so often that it could not be explained away as a mere coincidence.

From personal experiences, I know there are friendly Guides available to everyone who will recognize them and accept their services. In order to avail oneself of the services of these unseen Guides, two things are necessary; first, one must express gratitude for their services; second, *one must follow their guidance to the letter*. Neglect in this respect will bring sure, if not always swift, disaster. Perhaps this may explain why some people meet with disasters, the cause of which they cannot understand; disasters which they do not belive to be the results of any fault on their part.

For many years I was so sensitive concerning the unseen Guides, whose presence I had felt, that I carefully avoided all references to them, in both my writings and in public lectures. Then, one day in a conversation with Elmer R. Gates, a distinguished scientist and inventor, I was overwhelmed with joy when I learned that he not only had discovered the presence of unseen Guides, but he had formed a working alliance with them which enabled him to perfect more inventions and procure more patents than had ever been granted to the great inventor, Thomas A. Edison.

From that day on I began to make inquiries of the hundreds of successful men who collaborated with me in the organization of the Science of Success, and discovered that *each of them had received guidance from unknown sources,* although many of them were reluctant to admit this discovery. My experience with men in the upper brackets of personal achievements has been that they prefer to accredit their success to their *individual superiority*.

Thomas A. Edison, Henry Ford, Luther Burbank, Andrew Carnegie, Elmer R. Gates, and Dr. Alexander Graham Bell went to great lengths in their descriptions of their experiences with unseen Guides, although some of these men did not refer to these invisible sources of aid as "guides." Dr. Bell, in particular, believed the invisible source of aid was nothing but a direct contact with Infinite Intelligence, brought about by the individual's stimulation of his own mind through a burning desire for the attainment of definite objectives.

Through the guidance of unseen forces, Madame Marie Curie was directed to the revelation of the secret and the source of supply of radium, although she did not know in advance where to begin looking for the radium, or what it would look like if she found it.

Thomas A. Edison had an interesting view as to the nature and source of the invisible forces which he used so freely in his work of research in the field of invention. He believed that all thoughts released by all people at all times are picked up and become a part of the ether, where they remain forever, just as they were released by the individuals; that anyone may tune in and contact these previously released thoughts by conditioning the mind, through definiteness and clearness of purpose, to contact any desired type of thoughts which may be related to that purpose. For example, Mr. Edison discovered that when he concentrated his thoughts upon an idea he wished to perfect, he could "tune in" and pick up from the great reservoir of the boundless ether thoughts related to that idea which had been previously released by others who had thought along the same line.

Mr. Edison called attention to the fact that water runs its course, through rivers and streams, renders a great variety of services to mankind, and returns finally to the oceans from which it came, there to become a part of the main body of water, where it is cleansed and made ready to begin its journey all over again. This coming and going of water, without diminishing or increasing its quantity, has a definite parallel in the energy of thought.

Mr. Edison believed that the energy with which we think is a projected portion of Infinite Intelligence; that this Intelligence becomes specialized into myriad ideas and concepts through the brain of man, and when thoughts are released they return, like the water returns to the oceans, to the great reservoir from whence the energy came, and are there filed and classified so that all related thoughts are arranged together.

Mr. Edison definitely ruled out the belief of some who claim that the invisible Guides are departed people who once lived on earth. In this decision I fully concur, for I *have never found the slightest evidence that indicates that people who depart from the earth ever communicate with those who are living.* In fairness to those who may believe otherwise, I frankly admit that this is only my personal opinion; that the opinion was arrived at, not by evidence, *but for the lack of evidence.*

Turning back the pages of history of civilization, one cannot help but be profoundly impressed with the fact that always, when people have been overtaken by some great crisis which threatened to destroy the achievements of civilization, a leader has made his appearance with the necessary *inner wisdom* to provide the means of survival and continuation of civilization.

We had evidence that adequate leadership always appeared in times of great crises when the British threatened the freedom of the people of the Colonies in 1776, in the person of George Washington and his little army of underfed, underclothed, untrained and underarmed soldiers.

We had further evidence when this nation was being torn apart by inner strife, during the War Between the States, in the person of the great leader, Abraham Lincoln.

And we had still further evidence in World Wars I and II, when we were compelled to fight the combined forces of science, manned by barbarians who were out to destroy human rights and personal freedom all over the world.

In all such cases there always have appeared unseen forces and circumstances, which help RIGHT to prevail over WRONG.

And every individual is born with an accompanying group of unseen Guides sufficient to supply all his or her needs, and with these Guides come definite penalties for neglect to recognize and use them, also definite rewards for their recognition and use. In the main, the rewards consist in the necessary wisdom to insure the individual's success in carrying out his mission in life, whatever that may be, and to show him the way to the most priceless of all riches—*peace of mind.*

Throughout this volume I have described, through many phrases and illustrations, the Supreme Secret of all human achievements. Those who discover this secret will receive with it the means of recognizing and bringing into their service the unseen Guides which may now lie dormant, awaiting recognition and the call to service.

The presence of these Guides, and evidence of their active service in one's behalf, will be recognized by the improvements and benefits which will begin to manifest themselves from the very day the Guides receive recognition and are given *definite instructions*.

Fantastic and impractical, does someone exclaim?

No, "miraculous" is a better word, because no one, so far as I know, has yet explained the source of these unseen Guides, or how or why they are assigned to guide the lives of every living person. But there are thousands of people among the students of the Science of Success who know that the Guides exist because they too have learned the method—the Supreme Secret—by which this guidance can be acquired.

The unseen Guides are housed in that "other self" which every person possesses; that self which one does not see when looking into a mirror; that self which does not recognize the word "impossible," nor the limitations of any nature whatsoever; that self which is the master of all physical pain, all sorrow, defeat, and temporary failure.

Somewhere along the way, as you read this volume, your "other self" may jump out from behind the lines, where you can recognize it, if you have not already done so. When that point has been reached, turn down the page and mark it for future reference, for you will have come to a profound turning point of your life.

Nowhere in these remarks am I endeavoring to prove anything! I am only endeavoring to introduce the reader to that "other self" who, once it has been recognized, will provide all the proof anyone could desire. Which is only another way of saying I am trying to induce the reader to look "within" for the answer to the riddle of Life—to THINK for himself!

How to Give Instructions to Your "Other Self" While You Sleep

The time is nearing when one may treat physical ailment, master the inferiority complexes, and condition the mind for any desired purpose while one is asleep. Moreover, it will be possible to master any desired language, and acquire education on any subject while one sleeps.

These seemingly fantastic achievements will be attained through the aid of a specially built phonograph which will play back, every fifteen minutes while one is asleep, recordings giving scientifically prepared treatments on any subject, for any desired purpose. The machine has been perfected so it can be set with a time clock which will start the record playing after one is asleep.

The reason for this treatment while one sleeps is this: While one is awake the conscious section of the mind stands guard at the door through which the subconscious must be reached, and modifies or rejects outright all influences and instructions which one may endeavor to give the subconscious. And the conscious mind is a cynic of no small force. It seems to be more easily influenced by fear and suspicion and doubt than it is by positive influences. For this reason any directives one desires to give to the subconscious can best be given when the conscious mind is asleep and off duty.

The "other self" can be reached only through the subconscious mind, and this irresistible entity with which everyone is possessed is some mysterious power associated with, and existing on, the same plane as our unseen Guides.

This system of sleep treatment is especially adaptable to the purpose of developing sound traits of character and the elimination of undesirable habits in children, while they sleep, and it can be put into operation without the knowledge of the children.

All treatments in preparation for dentistry or surgical operations must be recommended by and taken under the supervision of one's local physician or dentist.

CHAPTER V

The Universal Language of Pain
The Third Miracle of Life

PHYSICAL PAIN is the universal language in which Mother Nature speaks to every creature on earth, and it is *understood and respected by all.* I have never known a normal minded person who did not dread physical pain. I have never known one who did not try, in every way possible, to avoid physical pain. However, pain is one of the cleverest of nature's devices, because it is the means by which she forces individuals in all degrees of intelligence to observe the law of self-preservation.

When physical pain calls, the individual responds and endeavors to remove the cause. If pain comes in the form of a headache, the intelligent individual generally looks for its cause, and quite often finds that it comes from toxic poisoning through inadequate elimination. A dose of salts or a enema gives immediate temporary relief.

If the less intelligent individual experiences a headache he is likely to swallow a few aspirin tablets and say, "There, now, I guess that will take care of the matter," which it usually does temporarily—not by correcting the cause, but by temporarily paralyzing the nerve which is carrying the warning cry of pain from the source of its origin to the brain, where something could and should be done about it.

When nature's gentler forms of pain fail to move the individual to heed the call and look into the cause, nature generally cuts him down and sends him to bed through a *fortunate* spell of sickness, while she gives him a complete physical repair job. The more intelligent person never speaks of sickness as a misfortune, but looks upon it as a blessing, a sort of merciful form of largess bestowed upon him by Mother Nature, through which he is given a new lease on life instead of a funeral.

Pain and physical ailments are curses only when they are regarded as such by those who do not recognize that they are devices for the good of man, without which no one could live out the customary three score and ten years.

When nature hospitalizes an individual, whether he goes to bed in a hospital or in his own home, she takes him out of action so that she may use all of his energies for self-restoration purposes. Also, she gives him a much needed rest and time to discover the power and usages of his own mind, as well as engage in meditation and thought *regarding the cause of his ailments.* Thus he may discover that the cause originated from a variety of sins which he might have avoided had he listened to the voice of pain.

Physical illness is so definitely a blessing that those who send cards of sympathy to their sick friends should send cards of congratulation instead, worded something like the following:

CONGRATULATIONS ON YOUR GOOD FORTUNE IN HAVING A BLESSED PERI- OD OF REST, ATTENDED BY THE GREATEST OF ALL DOCTORS—DOCTOR

TIME—WHO KNOWS WHAT YOU NEED
AND WILL SEE THAT YOU RECEIVE IT.

Take this *positive attitude* toward physical ailments and observe how well your mental attitude serves to remove the cause of your illness. Then you will recognize that physical pain and illness are blessings, without which man would not long survive.

Along with the universal language of pain, nature has ingeniously provided the means of endurance of the pain, and a stop-gap when the capacity for endurance has been reached, in the form of unconsciousness. When the pain reaches beyond human endurance one simply goes to sleep, in a state of unconsciousness.

There are two forms of pain. One is physical; the other is mental, existing only in the mind. Most physical pains are greatly exaggerated by one's mental reaction to them. In dentistry, for example, the pain is approximately ten percent physical and *ninety percent mental*. Most of the suffering in dentistry occurs in the form of fear, before the patient is seated in the dentist's chair. Modern dental technique has all but removed the actual physical pain of dental operations; and modern psychology, as shown in a subsequent chapter, has wiped out the mental pain of dentistry.

The mastery of physical pain poses one of the greatest challenges to those who are seeking peace of mind through self-discipline. It provides an unexcelled opportunity for one to *take full possession of his mind,* the one thing one must do in order to make life pay off on his own terms. Become the master over the appetite, by following the formula in a subsequent chapter—put the stomach under complete control—and mastery of the fear of physical pain will not be difficult.

The American Indians have always been without fear of physical pain. Originally, before the Indians were softened and corrupted by the coming of the white man, when they were wounded they continued to move around and engage in their daily labors as though nothing had happened. Taking their cue from the Indians, many surgeons now advise patients who have undergone certain types of surgical operations to go back to their daily routine of living very shortly after surgery. The surgeon recognizes, and so did the Indians perhaps, that nature does a wonderful job of healing when one depends upon her and learns how to cooperate with her intelligently.

In the mountain sections of the South there are women who give birth to babies one day and go back to their housework, or even to labor in the fields, the following day. They make no more to-do about childbirth than many women do about a headache or a cold; and *they know not the fear of physical pain!*

In battles, during war times, it is not unusual for men to keep on fighting after being badly wounded, oftentimes without realizing any pain until after the battle has ended. Under the stress of battle the soldier's mind is so fully concentrated on the job at hand that he rises above the fear of physical pain; *therefore he does not feel pain until his emotions slow down to normal.*

Taking our cue from the foregoing statement of known fact, it should be obvious that nature has provided us with a wonderful mechanism with which we may rise above physical or mental pain, and master every form of fear, as well as overcome sorrow and frustration of every nature. The precise formula through which this may be accomplished is clearly set forth in the chapter which describes how one may prepare the mind for dentistry.

During my forty odd years of experience in connection with the organization and the teaching of the Science of Success, I have had the privilege of coming into close contact with practically every known type of human problem and every type of human being. One of the impressive lessons I learned from these intimate contacts consisted in the fact that the more successful, *the truly great people,* the leaders in their chosen fields of endeavor, had mastered the fear of both physical and mental pain. Conversely, I observed that the failures and the never-do-wells were the victims of the fear of both physical and mental pain, very often to the point of superstition.

From this statement of fact it becomes apparent that there is a direct and significant relationship between the mastery of fear of physical and mental pain and the achievement of personal success in one's calling. And the significance is this: The mastery of physical and mental pain strongly indicates that one has taken complete charge of his own mind, *this being the one thing, and the only thing, over which the Creator provided man with the privilege of absolute control.*

During the course of my research into the causes of success and failure I conducted many classes in which were enrolled men and women in practically every walk of life. One of the most remarkable characters I ever knew was a widow who attended one of my classes in Washington, D.C. She lost her husband in World War I. Shortly thereafter she became ill and had to undergo a major surgical operation. The first operation was not successful and it had to be followed by two additional operations. The expenses of her illness made it necessary for her to sell her modest home. Therefore, when she left the hospital after the last operation she had no place to live. She had two sons who were married, but neither of the wives would permit her to live in their homes, even temporarily. She had one brother and one sister, neither of whom would take care of her while she convalesced from her illness.

Finally, the pastor of the church which she had previously attended took a hand and found a neighbor who gave her a temporary home. It was here that I met this remarkable woman for the first time, having been summoned with the hope that I might help her become self-supporting. Of course this was a charity case and I had no intention of making any charge for my services, but I got the surprise of my life when I told the woman I wished her to become my student without any charge for tuition. I consider her reply to my offer a classic, worthy of quoting here:

"You are very kind," she began, "but I have always believed there is no such reality as something for nothing.

"You are a professional man and you earn your living by teaching other people how to live properly. Therefore, I shall enter your class and place myself under your guidance, only with the distinct understanding that I am doing so under a deferred payment arrangement.

"It is true that I have suffered both physical pain and mental anguish, but I have not quit fighting; nor have I gone down under these trying circumstances. I have no financial means at present, but I do have all the faculties of my mind, and I intend to use these faculties, as the Lord intended I should, to make myself free from want and free from all manner of fear.

"I have lost my husband, but so have thousands of other women, and I am no better than they.

"My children and my brother and sister declined to give me a helping hand when I most needed it, but their refusal has injured them more than it did me, for it has deprived them of an opportunity to be merciful to a helpless person, and still left open a way by which I may regain my independence through the use of my own mind.

"I do not regret the suffering I have gone through because it has given me the moral stamina with which I shall gain for myself freedom in the future.

"And," she continued, "I do not hold any ill feeling against my family for refusing to come to my rescue, because their neglect has provided me with a wonderful opportunity to comply with the Lord's admonition to forgive those who injure us: *FORGIVE US OUR SINS AS WE FORGIVE THOSE WHO TRESPASS AGAINST US.*

"During the adversities through which I have passed I

have found the seed of an equivalent benefit. It consists in my discovery of the power of my own mind and the means by which that power can be made the master of sorrow and suffering.

"But, the most wonderful benefit I have received from my adversities consists in my discovery that suffering, whether it be from physical pain or mental anguish, *places one in a favorable position for appeal to the Lord.*

"Before my husband was killed I belonged to a church!

"After meeting with adversities without going down under them I have become a Christian, and I now *LIVE MY RELIGION,* INSTEAD OF MERELY ACCEPTING IT AS SOMETHING TO BELIEVE.

"Truly, in the hour of my greatest suffering I discovered my own invincible soul! Therefore, surely you can see why I hold no grudges against my relatives, for it was by their neglect more than anything else, that I was introduced to the powers of my own mind.

"I do not feel sorry for myself, but I do feel very sorry for my own flesh and blood because they were not ready to embrace a wonderful opportunity to discover the greatness of their own minds by the exercise of mercy toward one who had a right to expect help from them."

This woman entered my class, mastered the Science of Success, and later was appointed by the President of the United States to one of the highest positions in the government ever held by a woman. Later she began organizing women employees of the government in a class, where she taught them the way to discover their own minds, using as the basis of her instruction the Science of Success philosophy which represents all that is known of the fundamentals of self-determination.

Yes, it took something more than three major operations, the loss of a husband, the loss of her financial means, and the refusal of relatives to come to her aid in the time of need, to whip this brave woman who found the path to the source of all power, through adversity and suffering, both mentally and physically.

She found that "seed of an equivalent benefit" which came from her suffering, *solely by her positive mental attitude toward it!* She discovered the way to transmute negative circumstances into positive benefits—a privilege which is the right of every human being.

Suffering, through physical or mental pain, disappointments, frustrations, and sorrows, is the means by which one may become great or go down in permanent failure. The determining factor as to which of these two circumstances one embraces *depends entirely upon one's mental attitude toward them.* To one person they may become stumbling-blocks. To another person, such as the widow whose story you have read, they become stepping-stones to a higher plane of life, from which one may become the master of all he surveys.

The story of this widow would not be complete without the quotation of her favorite prayer:

"I ask not for over-abundance of material things, O Lord, but only for the things I need. And I ask not to be relieved from sorrow and pain, but only to be shown how to transmute these into wisdom through which to adapt myself to the overall plan and purpose of life on earth. And I ask for no favor which is not equally available to all mankind. Should I be injured by others I ask only that I may be given the strength to forgive; that they may be given the privilege to regret. Lastly, I ask only that I be guided in all the circumstances of my life so as to adapt myself to them favorably, through understanding."

Times without number, during the forty odd years I have devoted to the study of human behavior, I have observed men and women who found their spiritual estates because of physical or mental pain.

The greatest woman I have ever known, my stepmother, spent a large portion of her later life suffering almost unbearable pain from arthritis; yet she put into motion an undertaking which has already benefitted many millions of people and is destined to benefit yet untold millions, some of them as yet unborn. She was responsible for my early training which led eventually to my being commissioned by Andrew Carnegie to give the world its first practical philosophy of personal achievement.

Had my stepmother not been confined to a wheel chair, no one would have suspected she was in constant physical pain. Her voice was always pleasant and she conversed only in a positive trend of thought. She never complained, but always had a word of encouragement for all of us who lived close to her. I am sure that anyone who knew her, and understood the extent to which she had mastered physical pain, would have been utterly ashamed to have expressed fear of any form of dentistry or surgery. My stepmother's mental attitude toward physical pain was one of the major factors which made her a truly great person, loved by all who knew her, envied by some because of her profound self-discipline.

Thus we see, once again, that one's mental attitude toward physical pain is the determining factor which makes pain the master, or merely something to be transmuted into some form of beneficial service. Instead of thinking of her own physical pain and complaining about it, my stepmother *directed her mind to helping others*— particularly members of our family; and in that way minimized the effects of her suffering. This might prove a beneficial suggestion for all who allow their minds to dwell upon their own troubles.

And it might be helpful too if those who have problems they believe are without solution were convinced that the best possible way to solve such problems is to look around until one finds another person with a similar or greater problem, and helps that person find the solution to his own problem. By this means the negative mind is transferred from oneself and is transmuted into a positive mind which is directed for the benefit of others; and the chances are a thousand to one that by the time the other fellow's problem has been solved one will have found the solution to his own.

A positive mind is practically an irresistible power which one may direct to the attainment of any desired purpose, including of course the mastery of both mental pain and physical pain. Again may I remind you, a positive mind is also the first of the Twelve Great Riches of Life.

In a subsequent chapter the formula for the maintenance of a positive mind is clearly described. Master that formula, learn to apply it, and you will no longer fear either physical pain or mental pain. As a matter of fact, *you will no longer fear anything.* You will no longer bind yourself on a level of mediocrity by your self-imposed limitations, in connection with your occupation or any portion of your life. You will no longer need help from anyone, but rather you will be in a position to extend help to many.

Most people condemn themselves to prison all their lives, despite the fact that they carry the keys to their prison without knowing they possess them. The prison consists in the self-imposed limitations they set up in their own minds, or permit others to set up for them. The keys consist in the power everyone has been given by the Creator to take full possession of the mind and to direct it to the solution of all problems, the accomplishment of all desired ends.

Those who exercise this inexorable prerogative, and take full possession of their own minds, never fear anything, never limit themselves in the achievement of desired ends, *and they attract to themselves, with ease, an overabundance of everything that represents individual success.*

Remember, wherever that old carrion crow of fear hovers there is something asleep which needs to be awakened, or something dead which needs to be buried. It is one of the strangest anomalies of life that the absence of fear, and not formal education or brilliance of mind, *is the major cause of individual success*.

Fear, in any form, is not only the major stumbling block which brings failure in connection with one's calling, but fear is also the major reason why most prayers bring only negative results. The opposite of fear is Faith, and Faith is the master of everything which one does not want, the means of attaining everything one does desire.

The only thing which makes it possible for an individual to rise above the fear of any physical ailment is for him to recognize that he has a mind which is without limitations, except those he himself places upon it.

A little while ago the dentist who made my dentures was telling another patient of his how I went through dental surgery and had all of my teeth extracted without pain or discomfort. The patient was a clergyman, *yet he expressed doubt that anyone could do that*. I wonder what sort of a clergyman he really is. Most clergymen know that the power of the mind is *without limitation when it is stimulated by Faith*. And all physicians and dentists know that, in most cases, fear hurts the patient more than the physical ailment with which he suffers.

May I conjecture that physicians and dentists will welcome the coming of this book which teaches how to condition the mind for dentistry or surgery, so the patient will be free from fear. The book will be welcomed because it will lighten the burdens of the physicians and the dentists whose patients follow the counsel it presents, as well as relieve the patients of the suffering they experience through fear.

While it is true that physical pain is the universal language in which nature speaks to all living things, it is also true that with this language has been provided an ingenious device to insure that the individual can accept the guidance of pain without going down under it. When physical pain becomes greater than the individual can bear, nature puts him to sleep, which proves once more that nature maintains a balance in all things, *and never permits one to suffer any form of hurt or discomfort without providing the means of its cure.*

With this important knowledge of nature's ways as a starter, doctors have practically taken the fear of pain out of childbirth, through a system known as "twilight sleep," which reduces the patient to a state of semi-consciousness. Twilight sleep can be produced by mild hypodermic injections, which are without pain, or by treatment through suggestive therapeutics (partial hypnosis).

By the application of hypnosis, the conscious mind can be temporarily set aside and the doctor may then give his patient directives through the subconscious. Through this form of treatment, the subconscious can be given any directive which the individual may need to help him overcome physical pain or any mental condition that may be causing him distress, including of course *all forms of fear.*

Hypnosis is another of nature's clever safeguards which she has provided for the protection of the individual against both mental and physical pain, as well as a means by which the individual may condition his mind for the attainment of any desired objective, such as the substitution of opulence and financial prosperity to replace poverty.

Auto-suggestion (self-hypnosis) is being constantly used by all people, at all times, whether they recognize this fact or not, and the sad part of this truth is that most people unconsciously use this powerful device in a negative way so that it brings them poverty, ill health, unhappiness, fear, and self-imposed limitations in almost every conceivable form. This negative application of auto-suggestion takes place when an individual allows himself to be harassed by fears and worries which keep his mind *on the circumstances and things he does not desire.*

The positive application of auto-suggestion, through which one fixes his mind on the circumstances and things he desires, is more fully described in subsequent chapters. The formula by which this end is attained is simple and always under one's direct control.

When auto-suggestion is applied by two or more people who are working in perfect harmony for the attainment of a definite purpose, as in the case of a husband and wife during sexual engagement, the results often border on the miraculous.

As you progress in reading these chapters, there are certain important forces available for your use and benefit with which the author desires you to become fully familiar. Some of these are:

1. Auto-suggestion: The means by which one may give directives to the subconscious mind for any desired purpose, by the simple procedure of emotionalizing one's desires and repeating them often, as directed in later chapters.

2. Transmutation: The act of changing one form, substance or thought into another, such as the switching of the mind from thoughts of fear, unhappiness, and poverty to thoughts of affluence, happiness, and success. A powerful form of transmutation may occur when one begins to look for the "seed of an equivalent benefit" in all unpleasant circumstances, and directs his mind to the development of that seed instead of allowing the mind to brood over the circumstance which produced the seed.

3. The Master Mind: An alliance of two or more minds, in a state of perfect harmony, for the attainment of definite purposes. The most profound Master Mind alliance is that which may exist between a man and his wife.

4. Self-hypnosis: Hypnosis is a clever device, provided by nature, with which one may condition his mind for the attainment of any desired end. It is the means by which the individual may take possession of his own mind and direct it to either negative or positive ends. The privilege of control over the mind is the one and only thing over

which the Creator has given man the exclusive privilege of control, and auto-suggestion, or self-hypnosis, is the means by which this privilege can be made a curse or a blessing, according to the way one adopts and uses it.

Self-hypnosis is one of the major techniques by which the author has conditioned the minds of millions of people for the attainment of financial prosperity and peace of mind.

5. Subconscious: The subconscious section of the mind consists of a section of the brain which serves as the sixth sense, or the gateway to Infinite Intelligence. This gateway may be opened and used without limitation, for any desired purpose, through the aid of the formula presented in a subsequent chapter. It is by this gateway that all prayers must be presented. And, keep in mind always the important fact that it is through this gateway (which sometimes is carelessly left open) *that the negative thoughts released by other people may enter one's mind and cause failure, worry, defeat, and both mental and physical ailments.*

The sixth sense, operating through the subconscious mind, is both a broadcasting station and a receiving set for the vibrations of thought, and it is the individual's responsibility to safeguard himself against the negative thoughts of other people which this receiving set is constantly picking up, and also to protect other people by refraining from sending out over this broadcasting station any thoughts of a negative nature.

The only safe plan for the advancement of one's own welfare and the protection of others, is that of keeping the mind so busy broadcasting positive thoughts that no time is left for sending out negative thoughts, for it is as true as night follows day, *that whatever thoughts one sends out will come back greatly multiplied, to bless or to curse.*

A great philosopher stated this profound truth very succinctly when he said: "Whatever you do to or for another, by the thoughts you send forth, you do to or for *yourself."* Therefore, the best method of protecting oneself against the inflow of negative thoughts being released by other people is that of keeping the broadcasting station so busy sending out positive thoughts that no time will be available for receiving negative thoughts. This formula is unbeatable; it is practical, and *it is under the control of the individual.*

Negative thoughts released by other people can enter one's mind, through the sixth sense, but these can be instantly transmuted into positive thoughts and directed, through auto-suggestion, to the attainment of the circumstances and things one may desire. This is the most beneficial form of thought transmutation known to man, and one by which the individual may take full possession of his own mind.

Do not shy away from the terms "auto-suggestion" and "self-hypnosis" because you may not understand them. The simple truth is that you are constantly using these principles whether you recognize it or not. Therefore, instead of using them blindly, to destructive ends, it is better to embrace them and use them consciously for the attainment of desirable ends.

In this principle, which brings so many people to failure and defeat, consists also the potentials of triumph and success, when the principle is understood and applied with definiteness of purpose.

CHAPTER VI

Growth through Struggle
The Fourth Miracle of Life

THE NECESSITY FOR STRUGGLE is one of the clever devices through which nature *forces* individuals to expand, develop, progress, and become strong through resistance. Struggle can, and does, become either an ordeal or a magnificent experience through which the individual expresses gratitude for the opportunity to conquer the cause of his struggle.

Life, from birth until death, is literally an unbroken record of an ever increasing variety of struggles, which no individual can avoid.

Mastery of ignorance calls for struggle. Education involves eternal struggle, and every day is commencement day because education is cumulative. It is a lifetime job.

The accumulation of material riches abounds in the necessity for struggle; so much so in fact that many individuals actually kill themselves early in life due to anxiety and over-exertion in the effort to acquire more money than they need.

Maintenance of sound physical health calls for eternal

struggle with the multifarious enemies of sound health; struggle for food and shelter; struggle for an opportunity to earn a living; struggle to hold a job; struggle to gain recognition in a profession; struggle to keep a business out of bankruptcy.

Look in whatever direction we may, and we find that there is hardly a circumstance of daily life which does not call for individual struggle in order to survive.

We are forced to recognize that this great universal necessity for struggle must have a definite and useful purpose. That purpose is to force the individual to sharpen his wits, arouse his enthusiasm, build up his spirit of Faith, gain definiteness of purpose, develop his power of will, inspire his faculty of imagination to give him new uses for old ideas and concepts, and *thereby fulfill some unknown mission for which he may have been born.*

Struggle keeps man from going to sleep with self-satisfaction or laziness, and forces him onward and upward in the fulfillment of his mission in life, and he thereby makes his individual contribution to whatever may be the Universal Purpose of mankind on earth.

Strength, both physical and spiritual, is the product of struggle!

"Do the thing," said Emerson, "and you shall have the power."

Meet struggle and master it, says nature, and you shall have *strength and wisdom sufficient for all your needs.*

If you wish a strong arm, says nature, give it systematic use under the weight of a three-pound hammer and soon you will have muscles like bands of steel. If you do not wish a strong arm, says nature, tie it in a sling, take it out of use, and remove the cause for struggle, and its strength will wither and die.

In every form of life, atrophy and death come from idleness! The one thing nature will not tolerate is idleness. Through the necessity for struggle and the Law of Change nature keeps everything throughout the universe in a constant state of flux. Nothing, from the electrons and the protons of matter to the suns and planets which float throughout space, is ever still for a single second. Nature's motto is: Keep moving or perish! There is no halfway ground, no compromise, no exceptions for any reason whatsoever.

And should you doubt that nature intends every individual to keep struggling or perish, observe what takes place with the person who makes his fortune and "retires"—gives up the struggle because he no longer believes it is necessary.

The strongest trees are not those in heavily protected forests, but the trees which stand in open spaces where they are in constant struggle with wind and all the elements of weather.

My grandfather was a wagon maker. In clearing his land for the production of crops, he always left a few oaks standing in the open fields, where they could be toughened by exposure. These he later cut and used for the "fellows" needed in making wagon wheels—timber that could be bent into arc-shaped segments without breaking in the process. He found that trees protected by the forest could not produce the sort of timber he required. It was too soft and brittle because it had not been under the necessity for struggle—the self-same reason why some people are "soft" and unprepared to cope with the resistances of life.

Most people go through life by the line of least resistance in every circumstance where they can make a choice. They do not recognize *that following the line of least resistance makes all rivers, and some men, crooked!*

There may be some pain in most forms of struggle, but nature compensates the individual for the pain in the form of *power and strength and wisdom which come from practical experience.*

While organizing the Science of Success philosophy, I made the revealing discovery that all the more successful leaders, in every calling, in every profession, and every walk of life, had gained their leadership in almost exact ratio to the extent of their struggles in the attainment of their leadership.

I observed, with profound interest, that no man, who had not been thoroughly tested by the necessity of struggle, seemed ever to have been chosen as a leader in times of great crises during the interim between the stone age and our present day civilization.

Careful study of the entire record of civilization itself, from the age of the cave man to the present, shows clearly that it is the product of eternal struggle. Yes, struggle definitely is one of the Creator's devices for forcing individuals to respond to the Law of Change in order that the overall plan of the universe may be carried out.

When any individual reconciles himself to the state of mind wherein he is willing to accept largess from the government, instead of supplying his needs through personal initiative, that individual is on the road to decay and spiritual blindness. When a majority of the people of any nation give up their inherited prerogative right to make their own way through struggle, *history shows clearly that the entire nation is in a tailspin of decay that inevitably must end in extinction.*

The individual who not only is willing to live on the public treasury, *but demands that he be fed from it,* is already dead spiritually. The physical body still walks, but it is only an empty shell whose only hope for the future is a funeral. This, of course, has reference only to able-bodied people who quit the struggle because they are too indifferent or too lazy to keep on growing through the Law of Change and the urge for struggle.

For twenty odd years I was forced to struggle in mastering the problems incidental to my work in organizing the world's first practical philosophy of success. First, I was forced to struggle in preparing myself with the necessary knowledge to produce the philosophy. Secondly, I was forced to struggle to maintain myself economically while doing the research necessary to organize the philosophy. Then I met with still greater necessity for struggle while gaining recognition from the world for myself and the philosophy.

Twenty years of struggle without any direct financial compensation is an experience not calculated to give one sustained hope, but it was the price I had to pay for a philosophy which was destined to benefit untold numbers of people, many of whom were not born when I began my work.

Discouraging? Heartbreaking? Not at all, for I recognized from the beginning that out of my struggle would come triumph and victory in proportion to the labors invested in my task. In this hope I have not been disappointed, but I have been overwhelmed with the bountiful manner in which the world has responded and paid me tribute for the long years of struggle that went into my work.

Also, I have gained from my struggle something of still greater and more profound value. It is recognition that through my struggles I *have reached deeply into the spiritual wells of my soul,* and there I have found powers available for every purpose I may desire—powers I never knew I possessed, *and never would have discovered except by the means of struggle!*

Through my struggles I discovered, and learned how to make use of, the magical Eight Princes of Guidance described in a previous chapter—the unseen friends who administer to all of my physical, financial, and spiritual needs, who work for me while I sleep and while I am awake.

Also, it was through my struggles that the great Law of Cosmic Habitforce (the law that is the fixer of all habits, the comptroller of all natural laws) was revealed to me; the law which led me, at long last, to where I was ready to give the world the benefit of my experiences through struggle.

From my experiences with struggle I discovered that the Creator never singles out an individual for an important service to mankind without first testing him, through struggle, in proportion to the nature of the service he is to render. Thus, through struggle, I learned to interpret the laws, purposes, and working plans of the Creator as they related to me and to mankind in general.

What greater benefits could anyone desire from struggle?

What greater rewards could anyone gain from any other cause?

Briefly we have reviewed only four of Life's Miracles, but these are by no means the more important of the miracles we are to inspect on our trip through Nature's Wonderland Valley.

However, we have witnessed enough on our trip to convince us that there is good in all circumstances which touch or influence our lives, whether they be circumstances over which we have complete control or those over which we have no control *except the control of our mental reaction to them.*

As we proceed on our trip, through the chapters to follow, our minds should unfold until we recognize that circumstances which we may regard as unpleasant may be a part of the Creator's overall plan in connection with human destiny on this earth. The major purpose of this chapter is to broaden the mind so it may encompass and envision important facts of life *outside of those which immediately concern* the individual.

Peace of mind is not possible without this capacity for panoramic vision of the entire picture and purpose of life. We must recognize that our individual incarnation, through which we are tossed into this material world without ceremony and without our consent, was for a purpose above and beyond our individual pleasures and desires.

Once we understand this broader purpose of life we

become reconciled to the experiences of struggle we must undergo while passing this way, and we accept them as circumstances of opportunity through which we may prepare ourselves for still higher and better planes of existence than the one on which we now dwell.

CHAPTER VII

The Mastery of Poverty
The Fifth Miracle of Life

POVERTY is the result of a negative condition of the mind, which practically every living person experiences at one time or another. It is the first and the most disastrous of the seven basic fears, but it is only a state of mind, and like the other six fears, it is subject to the control of the individual.

The fact that a major portion of all people are born in surroundings of poverty, *accept it as inescapable,* and go with it all through their lives, indicates how potent a factor it is in the lives of people. It may well be that poverty is one of the testing devices with which the Creator separates the weak from the strong, for it is a notable fact that those who master poverty, become rich not only in material things, *but also rich and often wise in spiritual values as well.*

I have observed that men who have mastered poverty invariably have a keen sense of Faith in their ability to master practically everything else which stands in the way of their progress; while those who have accepted poverty as inescapable show signs of weakness in many other directions. In no case have I known anyone who had accepted poverty as unavoidable, who had not failed also to exercise that great Gift of the power to take possession of his own mind-power (as the Creator intended all people should do).

All people go through testing periods throughout their lives, under many circumstances, which clearly disclose whether or not they have accepted and used that Great Gift of exclusive control over their own mind-power. And I have observed that along with this Great Gift from the Infinite go also definite penalties for neglect to embrace and use the Gift, and definite rewards for its recognition and use.

One of the more important rewards for its use consists in complete freedom from the entire seven basic fears and all the lesser fears, with full access to the magic power of FAITH to take the place of these fears.

The penalties for neglect to embrace and use this Great Gift are legion. In addition to all of the seven basic fears, there are many other liabilities not included with these fears. One of the major penalties for failure to use the Great Gift is *the total impossibility of attaining peace of mind.*

Poverty has many merits if and when an individual relates himself to it in a positive mental attitude instead of submitting to it in the false belief that it is unavoidable, or the lazy attitude that it is not worth fighting off. Poverty may be one of the devices with which the Creator forces man to sharpen his wits, arouse his enthusiasm, act on his personal initiative and make a determined fight against the forces which oppose him, in order that he may survive.

Poverty may also be a device of the Creator by which he maneuvers man into a state of mind where he finally *discovers himself from within.* In a great country like the United States of America there is no valid reason for any able-minded person to accept and become bound to slavery through poverty. Here, as nowhere else in the world, is a training ground for personal freedom, which offers every individual the best of all possible opportunities to embrace and use this Great Gift of the *right to pattern his own earthly destiny and attain it*. And here, as nowhere else, has the individual been provided with every conceivable motive for embracing and using the Great Gift. The payoff is so great that the individual may literally "write his own ticket."

The best evidence that Destiny smiles on those who are born to poverty consists in the well-recognized fact that too seldom does an individual who is born to great wealth ever contribute any worthy contributions to the world which make it a better place for mankind. Many children of very rich people, who never have the benefit of the seasoning influence of poverty or struggle, often grow up "soft" and lacking in the necessary endurance or the motive to make themselves useful.

When fortune does smile upon a person who has great wealth she generally chooses only those who created their wealth through useful service—not those who inherited it or procured it through means which brought injury to others. Fortune definitely frowns upon all ill-gotten wealth, *and often causes it to mysteriously evaporate*.

Whether poverty becomes a curse or a blessing depends entirely upon the way the individual relates himself to it. If it is accepted in a spirit of meekness, as an unavoidable handicap, then it becomes just that. If poverty is accepted as a mere challenge to the individual to fight his way through and master, then it becomes a blessing—in fact, one of the great miracles of life. Poverty may become either a stumbling-block or a stepping-stone on which he may rise to whatever heights of achievement he may set his heart upon, depending entirely on his attitude toward it and his *reactions to it*.

Both poverty and riches consist in a state of mind! They follow precisely the pattern the individual creates and visualizes by the dominating thoughts he expresses. Thoughts of poverty attract their material counterpart. Thoughts of riches likewise attract their material counterpart. The law of *harmonious attraction* translates all thoughts into their kindred material counterparts. This great truth explains why the majority of people experience unhappiness and poverty throughout their lives. They allow their minds to fear unhappiness and poverty, and their dominating thoughts are on these circumstances. The law of harmonious attraction takes over and brings them *that which they expect*.

When I was a small boy I heard a very dramatic speech on the subject of poverty which made a lasting impression upon my mind, and I am sure that speech was responsible for my determination to master poverty despite the fact that I had been born in poverty and had never known anything expect poverty. The speech came from my stepmother shortly after she came to our home and took over one of the most forlorn, poverty-stricken places I have ever known.

The speech was as follows:

"This place which we call home is a disgrace to all of us and a handicap for our children. We are all able-bodied people and there is no need for us to accept poverty when we know that it is the result of nothing but laziness or indifference.

"If we stay here and accept the conditions under which we now live, our children will grow up and accept these conditions also. I do not like poverty; I have never accepted poverty as my lot, and I shall not accept it now!

"For the moment I do not know what our first step will be in our break for freedom from poverty, but this much I do know—we shall make that break successfully, no matter how long it may take or how many sacrifices we may have to make. I intend that our children shall have the advantage of good educations, *but more than this, I intend that they shall be inspired with the ambition to master poverty.*

"Poverty is a disease which, once it is accepted, becomes a fixation which is hard to shake off.

"It is no disgrace to be born in poverty but it most decidedly is a disgrace to accept this birthright as irrevocable.

"We live in the richest and the greatest country civilization has yet produced. Here opportunity beckons to everyone who has the ambition to recognize and embrace it, and as far as this family is concerned, if opportunity does not beckon to us, *we shall create our own opportunity to escape this sort of life.*

"Poverty is like creeping paralysis! Slowly it destroys the desire for freedom, strips one of the ambition to enjoy better things of life, and undermines personal initiative. Also, it conditions one's mind for the acceptance of myriad fears, including the fear of ill health, the fear of criticism and the fear of physical pain.

"Our children are too young to know the dangers of accepting poverty as their lot, but I shall see to it that they are made conscious of these dangers, and I shall see to it also that they become prosperity conscious, *that they expect prosperity and become willing to pay the price of prosperity.*"

I have quoted this speech from memory, but it is substantially what my stepmother said to my father in my presence shortly after they were married. That "first step" in the break from poverty, which she mentioned in her speech, came when my stepmother inspired my father to enter Louisville Dental College and become a dentist, and paid for his training with the life insurance money she received from the death of her first husband.

With the income from that investment in my father, she sent her three children and my younger brother through college and started each of them on the road to mastery of poverty.

As for myself, she was instrumental in placing me in a position where the late Andrew Carnegie gave me an opportunity such as no other author ever received—an opportunity which permitted me to learn from more than five hundred of the top-ranking, successful men who collaborated with me in giving the world a practical philosophy of personal achievement. A philosophy based on the "know-how" of my collaborators, gained from their lifetime experiences.

While it is estimated that my personal contribution to posterity has benefitted many millions of people, throughout two-thirds of the world, the credit for this accomplishment really dates back to that historic speech of my stepmother's, in which she disavowed poverty.

We see, therefore, that poverty can be the means of inspiring one to plan and achieve profound objectives. My stepmother did not fear poverty, but she disliked it and refused to accept it. And somehow the Creator seems to favor those who *know precisely what they want and what they do not want.* My stepmother was one of that type. If she had accepted poverty, or had she feared poverty, the lines you are now reading never would have been written.

Poverty is a great experience, but it is something to experience and then master before it breaks the will to be free and independent. The person who has never experienced poverty is to be pitied, perhaps, but the person who has experienced poverty and has accepted it as his lot is more to be pitied, for he has thereby condemned himself to eternal bondage.

Most of the truly great men and women throughout civilization have known poverty, but they experienced it, renounced it, mastered it and made themselves free. Otherwise they never would have become great. Anyone who accepts from life anything he does not want is not free. The Creator has provided everyone with the means of determining very largely his own earthly destiny, which consists in the privilege of freeing himself from those things which are not desirable.

Poverty can be a profound blessing. It can also be a lifelong curse. The determining factor as to which it shall be consists in one's mental attitude toward it. If it is accepted as a challenge to greater effort, it is a blessing. If it is accepted as an unavoidable handicap, then it is an enduring curse.

Remember that the *fear* of poverty brings with it a flock of related fears, including the fear of physical and mental pain.

A story was told of a man who died and went to hell. During his entrance examinations Satan asked, "What do you fear most?" To which the man replied, "I fear nothing."

"Then," returned Satan, "you are in the wrong place. *We accommodate only customers who are bound by fears.*"

Think of it! No place in hell for the person who has no fears.

I never hear the word "fear" that I do not think of a story told me by Reuben Darby, of the Massachusetts Mutual Life Insurance Company. When he was a small lad his uncle operated a grist mill on a Maryland plantation, on which a tenant family of Negroes lived. One day a ten-year-old child of the Negro family was sent down to the mill to request fifty cents of the plantation owner.

The owner looked up from his work, saw the Negro child standing at a respectful distance, and demanded, "What do you want?" Without moving from her tracks the child replied, "My mammy say send her fifty cents."

In a threatening tone of voice and a scowl on his face, the owner of the mill gruffly answered: "I'll do nothing of the sort! Now you run on back home, or I will take a switch to you," and he continued with his work.

In a little while he looked up again and saw the child still standing there. He grabbed a barrel stave, waved it toward the child, and said, "If you don't get out of here I'll use this on you. Now get going before I—" But he did not finish the sentence, for by that time the Negro child darted over in front of him, stuck her face up toward him, and screamed at the top of her voice, "My mammy's gotta have fifty cents!"

Slowly the mill owner laid down the barrel stave, reached into his pocket, pulled out fifty cents, and handed it to the child. She grabbed the money, quickly backed to the door, opened it, and then ran like a deer, while the mill owner stood with wide open eyes and mouth, pondering over the mysterious experience by which a Negro child had subdued him and got away with it—*something Negroes on his place were not supposed to do*.

Verily, fear can be transmuted into courage—a fact which the child demonstrated most convincingly.

Likewise, poverty can be transmuted into opulence and noteworthy achievements—a fact which my stepmother dramatically demonstrated by lifting our family out of both poverty and despair. She recognized that no person *who takes possession of his own mind and directs it to definite ends* needs to remain the victim of poverty, or of anything else he does not desire.

The difference between poverty and riches is not measurable in money or material possessions alone. There are twelve great riches, eleven of which are not material, but they are closely related to the spiritual forces available to mankind. In order that one may get a better idea of how to go about transmuting poverty into riches, the twelve great riches are here briefly described.

The Twelve Great Riches of Life

Grade yourself: Perfect, Fair, or Poor

1. A POSITIVE MENTAL ATTITUDE . . . .——
A positive Mental Attitude heads the list of the Twelve

Great Riches, because all riches, material or otherwise, begin as a state of mind, the one and only thing over which an individual has complete, inalienable powers of control. One's mental attitude supplies the "pulling power" which attracts to him the material equivalent of all fears, desires, doubts and beliefs. Mental attitude is also the factor which determines whether one's prayers bring negative or positive results. It is but little cause for wonder, therefore, that a Positive Mental Attitude heads the list of all the great riches of life.

2. SOUND PHYSICAL HEALTH. . . . .———

Sound health begins with a "health consciousness," the product of a mind which thinks in terms of health and not in terms of illness, plus temperance and moderation in eating, and in the balancing of physical activities. Maintenance of a Positive Mental Attitude is one of the greatest forms of prevention of ill health known to mankind. It rates as "great" because it is under one's control and is subject, at all times, to one's direction to any desired end.

3. HARMONY IN HUMAN RELATIONS. .———

There are two forms of harmony, both of which are required to entitle harmony to rank as one of the twelve great riches of life; namely, harmony with oneself and harmony with others. One's first responsibility is that of establishing harmony *within*. This calls for the mastery of fear, maintenance of a positive mental attitude, and the adoption of a major purpose in life, behind which one can build an enduring faith in its achievement. Be at peace within your own soul and you will have no difficulty in relating yourself in a spirit of harmony with others. Friction in human relations is often the result of confusion, frustration, fear, and doubt within the individual who, oftentimes, mirrors these negative states of mind in other people, thus making harmony impossible.

Harmony with others begins with harmony with one's self, for it is true, as Shakespeare said, "To thine own self be true, and it must follow, as the night the day, thou canst not then be false to any man." There are great benefits available to those who comply with his admonition.

4. FREEDOM FROM FEAR............ ———

No man enslaved by fear is rich; nor is he free. Fear is a harbinger of evil, an insult to the Creator who provided man with the means of rejecting all whatsoever which are not desired, by giving man complete control over his mind-power. Before grading yourself on Freedom From Fear, be sure to probe deeply into your soul and make certain that not one of the seven basic fears is hiding within you. And remember, when these seven basic fears have been transmuted into faith, you will have arrived at the point in your life where you can take possession of your own mind, *and through that possession acquire all you desire in life, as well as reject all you do not desire.* Without this Freedom From Fear, the other eleven riches of life may be useless.

In a subsequent chapter you will find the formula by which you can conquer the fear of ill health and physical pain. Apply the formula and conquer this fear; then follow through and conquer the other six basic fears with the same formula.

5. THE HOPE OF FUTURE
ACHIEVEMENT .... ———

Hope is the forerunner of the greatest of all states of mind, Faith! Hope sustains one in times of emergency when, without it, fear would take over. Hope is the basis of the most profound form of happiness which comes from the expectancy of success in some, as yet unattained, plan or purpose. Poor indeed is the person who cannot look toward the future with the hope that he will become the person he would like to be, or attain the position he would like to hold in life, or attain the objective he has failed to acquire in the past. Hope keeps the soul of man alert and active in his behalf, *and clears the line of communication by which Faith connects one with Infinite*

Intelligence. Hope is a right royal person and the Divine Decorator of the other eleven riches of life.

6. THE CAPACITY FOR FAITH........ ─────

Faith is the means of communication between the conscious mind of man and the great universal reservoir of Infinite Intelligence. It is the fertile soil of the garden of the human mind, wherein may be produced all the riches of life. It is the "eternal elixir" which gives creative power and action to the impulses of thought. It is the *élan vital* of the soul and it is without limitations. Faith is the spiritual quality which, when mixed with prayer, gives one direct and immediate connection with Infinite Intelligence. Faith is the power which transmutes the ordinary energies of thought into their spiritual equivalent, and it is the only means by which Infinite Intelligence may be appropriated to the uses of man.

7. WILLINGNESS TO SHARE ONE'S BLESSINGS .... ─────

He who has not learned the blessed art of sharing his blessings with others has not found the true path to enduring happiness, for happiness comes mainly from sharing of one's self and one's blessings. Let it be remembered that the space one occupies in the hearts of others is determined precisely by the service he renders through some form of sharing. Let it also be remembered that all riches may be embellished and multiplied by the simple process of sharing them where they may serve others. Neglect or refusal to share one's blessings is a sure way to cut the line of communication between a man and his soul. A great teacher said, *"The greatest among you is he who becomes the servant of all."* Another philosopher said, "Help thy brother's boat across, and lo! thine own hath reached the shore." And still another great philosopher said, "Whatsoever you do to or for another, you do to or for yourself."

8. A LABOR OF LOVE................. ─────

There can be no richer man than he who has found a

labor of love and is busily engaged in performing it, for a labor of love is the highest form of expression of human desires. Labor is the liaison between the demand and the supply of all human needs, the forerunner of all human progress, the medium by which the imagination of man is given wings of action. And all labor of love is sanctified because it brings joy of self-expression to him who performs it. Do the thing you like best and your life will be thereby enriched, your soul will be embellished, and you will be an inspiration for hope and faith and encouragement to all with whom you come into contact. Engagement in a labor of love is the greatest of all cures for melancholy, frustration, and fear. And it is a builder of physical health without equal.

9. AN OPEN MIND ON ALL SUBJECTS. .————

Tolerance, which is among the higher attributes of culture, is expressed only by the person who holds an open mind on all subjects, toward all people, at all times. And only the person who maintains an open mind becomes truly educated, and is thus prepared to embrace and use the twelve great riches of life. A closed mind atrophies and cuts off the line of communication between an individual and Infinite Intelligence. An open mind keeps the individual eternally in the process of education and the acquisition of knowledge with which he may take possession of his mind and direct it to the attainment of any desired purpose.

10. SELF-DISCIPLINE . . . .————

The person who is not the master of himself may never become the master of anything outside of himself. He who is the master of self may become the master of his own earthly destiny, and the "Master of his Fate, the Captain of his Soul." The highest form of self-discipline consists in the expression of humility of the heart when one has attained great riches, or has been blessed with widespread recognition for services rendered.

Self-discipline is the only means by which one may take full and complete possession of his own mind and direct it to the attainment of whatsoever ends he may wish.

11. THE CAPACITY TO UNDERSTAND PEOPLE ....——

The person who is rich in the understanding of people recognizes that all people are fundamentally alike, in that they have evolved from the same stem; that all human activities, good or bad, are inspired by one or more of the nine basic motives of life, namely:

(a) The emotion of LOVE

(b) The emotion of SEX

(c) The desire for MATERIAL GAIN

(d) The desire for SELF-PRESERVATION

(e) The desire for FREEDOM OF BODY AND MIND

(f) The desire for RECOGNITION and SELF-EXPRESSION

(g) The desire for PERPETUATION OF LIFE AFTER DEATH

(h) The emotion of ANGER

(i) The emotion of FEAR (See the seven basic fears)

The man who would understand others must first understand himself, for the motives which inspire him to action are, in the main, the same motives which would inspire others to action under the same conditions.

The capacity to understand others is the basis of all friendships; it is the basis of all harmony and cooperation among people, and the fundamental of greatest importance in all forms of leadership which call for friendly cooperation. Some people believe it is an approach of major importance in the understanding of the overall plan of the universe and the Creator thereof.

Know yourself and you will be well on the road to understanding others.

12. ECONOMIC SECURITY (Money)..... ———

The last, but not the least in importance, is the tangible portion of the twelve great riches, money, or the knowledge with which to insure one's economic security. Economic security is not attained by the possession of money alone. It is attained by the service one renders, for useful service may be converted into all forms of human needs, with or without the use of money.

Henry Ford attained economic security, not necessarily because he accumulated a vast fortune in money, but for the better reason that he provided profitable employment for millions of men and women, as well as dependable automobile transportation for still greater numbers of people.

Men and women who master and apply the Science of Success have economic security because they possess the means by which money can be acquired. They may run out of money, or lose it through poor judgment, but this does not deprive them of economic security, because they know the source of money and how to contact and benefit by that source.

Andrew Carnegie, who was perhaps the richest man in the world of his time, sponsored the organization of the Science of Success because he believed that the "know-how" of the accumulation of money should be known to everyone. During the latter portion of his life, Andrew Carnegie gave away most of his vast fortune of almost a billion dollars, but in a conversation with me shortly before he died, he said:

"I have given most of my fortune back to the people from whence it was accumulated, but the money I have given away is infinitesimally small in comparison with the riches I am leaving to the people in the 'know-how' of success, which I have entrusted to you for delivery to the world."

You now have an understanding of the antithesis of poverty in the twelve great riches of life. And it should be encouraging to observe that the first eleven of these riches are within the reach of all who will embrace them; and those who do embrace and use them will easily attract the twelfth of the riches, money.

Here, then, is the means by which poverty may be transmuted into riches, including all twelve of the great riches of life.

Embrace the twelve great riches, apply them in your daily life and you will become a success—for success is nothing more nor less than the attainment of these twelve blessings.

CHAPTER VIII

Failure May Be a Blessing
The Sixth Miracle of Life

FAILURE often becomes a blessing in disguise, because it turns people back from contemplated purposes which, had they been carried out, would have meant embarrassment or even total destruction. Failure often opens new doors of opportunity and provides one with useful knowledge of the realities of life, through the trial and error method. Failure often reveals the methods which will not work, and cures vain people of their conceits.

Failure of the British armies under Lord Cornwallis in 1781 not only gave the American Colonies their freedom, but probably saved the British Empire from total destruction in World Wars I and II.

The economic failures of the South, due to the loss of their slaves in the Civil War, eventually yielded the seed of an equivalent benefit in more ways than one:

1. The loss of slaves forced people to begin depending

upon themselves, and thereby they developed personal initiative.

2. The loss forced the women of the South to become independent by taking their places alongside of men in business and in the professions.

3. And, at long last, American industry is rapidly moving southward, where labor, raw materials, fuel, and weather conditions are more favorable. Thanks to the personal initiative of the Southerners, they stopped hating the Yankees and began to sell the South to northern industry.

In due time the South may become the industrial center of the United States.

Dr. Alexander Graham Bell spent years of research looking for the means of creating a mechanical hearing aid for his hard-of-hearing wife. In his original purpose he failed, but the research yielded the secret of the long-distance telephone.

When radio first came into popularity, about 1920, the Victor Talking Machine Company became frightened because it appeared that radio would ruin the talking machine business. The chief engineer of the Victor Talking Machine Company discovered, *in the principle of radio itself*, the means by which better recordings could be made, and from that discovery was born a demand for talking machines, such as the company never would have known without the discovery.

Thomas A. Edison's first major failure came when his teacher sent him home from school with a note advising his parents that he could not take an education. This so shocked Edison that he acquired an education which enabled him to become a truly great inventor.

Also, Edison's partial deafness might have been considered by some people as a failure of major proportions, but he adapted himself to it in such a way that he developed the power to hear "from within," through his sixth sense.

This was a strong factor perhaps in his ability to uncover so many of nature's secrets in his business of inventing.

The loss of my mother, who died when I was a very young lad, would have been considered by some people a handicap of major proportions, but it turned out differently. I was compensated for the loss of my mother with a stepmother whose influence upon me was so profound that she inspired me to engage in a calling whereby I have been able to serve others to a far greater extent than I might otherwise have done.

I felt that I had met with a major failure when a great uncle who was a multi-millionaire (after whom I was named) died and left no portion of his fortune to me. I later had reason to be thankful I was left out of his will, for it became necessary for me to master poverty on my own account, through my own initiative, *and in doing so I learned the way to teach others how to master poverty*.

Analyze failure under whatsoever circumstances you choose and you will discover the profound truth that every failure brings with it the seed of an equivalent benefit. This does not mean that failure brings with it the full ripened fruit of an equivalent benefit, but only the seed which must be discovered, germinated and developed to fruition through one's personal initiative, imagination, and definiteness of purpose.

Most men would consider the loss of the use of their legs a failure of major proportions, but Franklin D. Roosevelt so related himself to such a loss that it gave him a determined spirit to get along with braces, and he seemed to have done very well for himself without the use of his legs. His *mental attitude* toward his affliction was such that he reduced his handicap to a minimum of inconvenience.

The failures of Abraham Lincoln in store-keeping, surveying, soldiering and the practice of law, turned his talents in a direction which prepared him to become the greatest President the United States has ever known.

More than twenty major failures which I experienced during the early part of my career changed my path and guided me eventually into a field in which I can best serve others.

Clarence Saunders' failure as a store clerk yielded him an idea from which he made a profit of four million dollars in four years. That idea was the Piggly-Wiggly System of self-help grocery stores, which marked the beginning of the self-help store system now in operation on a widespread scale throughout the country.

Failure in physical health often diverts attention of the individual from his physical body to his brain power, and introduces him to the real "boss" of the physical body—the mind—and opens wide horizons of opportunity which he never would have known without the failure of health.

Milo C. Jones of Fort Atkinson, Wisconsin, made a bare living from his farm until he was stricken with paralysis and suffered total loss of the use of his body. Then he made a discovery which only such an affliction could have uncovered for him. He discovered that he had a mind and its possibilities of achievement were limited only by his desires and demands upon it, even without the use of his physical body. Through the aid of his mind he conceived the idea of making sausage from young hogs, named his product "Little Pig Sausage," and lived to become a multi-millionaire.

The fact that Mr. Jones did not discover his fabulous source of riches while he had the full use of his physical body is something which provides food for profound thought. The great Law of Change had to throw Milo C. Jones flat on his back and break up his old habits, by which he earned his living with his hands, in order to introduce him to his brain power, which he discovered to be infinitely greater than his brawn power.

Verily, nature never permits an individual to be deprived of any of his inborn rights and blessings without providing him with the potentials of an equivalent benefit in some form, as in the case of Milo C. Jones.

Failure is a blessing or a curse, depending upon the individual's reaction to it. If one looks upon failure as a sort of nudge from the Hand of Destiny which signals him to move in another direction, and if he acts upon that signal, the experience is practically sure to become a blessing. If he accepts failure as an indication of his weakness and broods over it until it produces an inferiority complex, then it is a curse. *The nature of the reaction* tells the story, and this is under the exclusive control of the individual always.

No one has complete immunity against failure, and everyone meets with failure many times during a lifetime, but everyone also has the privilege and the means by which he can react to failure in any manner he pleases.

Circumstances over which one has no control may, and they sometimes do, result in failure, but there are no circumstances which can prevent one from reacting to failure in a manner best suited for his benefit.

Failure is an accurate measuring device by which an individual may determine his weaknesses; and it provides therefore an opportunity for correcting them. In this sense failure always is a blessing.

Failure usually affects people in one or the other of two ways: It serves only as a challenge to greater effort or it subdues and discourages one from trying again.

The majority of people give up hope and quit at the first signs of failure, even before it overtakes them. And a large percentage of people quit when they are overtaken by a single failure. The potential leader is never subdued by failure, but is always inspired to greater effort by it. Watch your failures and you will learn whether you have potentialities for leadership. Your reaction will give you a dependable clue.

If you can keep on trying after three failures in a given undertaking you may consider yourself a "suspect" as a potential leader in your chosen occupation. *If you can keep on trying after a dozen failures the seed of a genius is germinating within your soul.* Give it the sunshine of Hope and Faith and watch it grow into great personal achievements.

It appears that nature often knocks individuals down with adversities in order to learn who among them *will get up and make another fight!* Those who make the grade are chosen as people of destiny, to serve as leaders in work of great importance to mankind.

May I remind you that the next time you meet with failure, if you will remember that every failure and every adversity carries with it the seed of an equivalent benefit, and start where you stand to recognize that seed and begin to germinate it through action, you may discover that *there never is any such reality as failure until one accepts it as such!*

It would have been most natural and logical for Milo C. Jones to have accepted his affliction as a knockout blow from which he never would recover, and no one would have blamed him if he had done so, but he reacted to his handicap in a positive manner which yielded him a better working relationship with the power of his mind. His *reaction* was the important part of the experience, because it paid off in terms of financial riches such as he had never dreamed of acquiring.

Most so-called failures are only temporary defeats which can be converted into assets of a priceless nature if one takes a positive mental attitude toward them.

From birth until death, Life poses a constant challenge to people to master failure without going down for the count, and rewards with bountiful opulence and great personal powers those who successfully meet the challenge.

The world generously forgives one for his mistakes and temporary defeats, provided always he accepts them as such and keeps on trying, *but there is no forgiveness for the sin of quitting when the going is hard!*

Life's motto is: "A WINNER NEVER QUITS AND A QUITTER NEVER WINS!"

Japan's failure in World War II was her greatest victory, since that failure broke the vicious yoke of superstition by which the Japanese people had been bound, and gave them their first taste of democracy and an opportunity to take their place in the family of civilized peoples on an equality with all others.

In all human endeavors nature seems to favor the "fool" who did not know he could fail, but who went ahead and did the "impossible" before he discovered it couldn't be done.

Henry P. Kaiser had never built seaworthy ships, but the emergency of World War II called for more ships than the established ship-building sources could supply, so Mr. Kaiser began building ships with such faith and enthusiasm that he literally "ran rings" around some of the older and more experienced men in that business, with an all-time high in production and all-time low in cost!

The man who says "it can't be done" usually winds up under the feet of the man who is busy doing it—*the man who succeeds because he has thrown himself in the path of the laws of the universe and adapted himself to their habits,* and thereby insured himself against failure. The man who says "it can't be done" has never studied nature's laws.

An old miner spent thirty years in search of precious metals, only to meet with disappointment and despair until he was overtaken by the misfortune of having his trusty mule break its leg in a gopher hole. The mule had to be shot. While digging a hole in which to bury the animal the miner struck the richest copper deposit in the entire world!

Destiny often selects dramatic ways in which to reward

people for stick-to-itiveness and the will to keep on trying in the face of defeat.

In this world of practical realism one must constantly remind himself that *our only limitations are those which we set up in our minds or permit others to establish for us.*

Henceforth and forever remember that no experience can be classified as a failure unless and until it has been accepted as such! Remember also, that only the person who meets with a given experience has the right to call it a failure, or some other name; that the verdict of all others is ruled out.

Fifty-Four Major Causes of Failure

1. The habit of drifting with circumstances, without definite aims or purposes.
2. Unfavorable physical heredity at birth.
3. Meddlesome curiosity in connection with other people's affairs.
4. Lack of a Definite Major Purpose as a life goal.
5. Inadequate schooling.
6. Lack of self-discipline, which generally manifests itself through excesses in eating, drinking and sex indulgence, and indifference toward opportunities for self-advancement.
7. Lack of ambition to aim above mediocrity.
8. Ill health, generally due to wrong thinking, improper diet, and lack of physical exercise. (Keep in mind, however, that some people, such as Helen Keller, have made themselves of great service to others despite incurable ailments.)
9. Unfavorable environmental influences during childhood. It has been said that the major fundamentals of character have been well formed in the individual by the time he is seven years of age.

10. Lack of persistence in carrying through to a finish that which one starts.
11. A negative mental attitude as a fixation of habit.
12. Lack of control over the emotions of the heart.
13. Desire for something for nothing, usually expressed in the habit of gambling.
14. Failure to reach decisions promptly and definitely and to stand by them after they have been made.
15. One or more of the seven basic fears.
16. Wrong selection of a mate in marriage.
17. Over-caution in business and professional relationships.
18. Lack of all forms of caution.
19. Wrong choice of associates in business or professional pursuits.
20. Wrong selection of a vocation, or total neglect to make a choice.
21. Lack of concentration of effort on the task at hand at a given time.
22. Habit of indiscriminate spending, without a budget control over income and expenditures.
23. Failure to budget and use TIME to best advantage.
24. Lack of *controlled* enthusiasm.
25. Intolerance—a closed mind based particularly on ignorance or prejudice in connection with religious, political, and economic subjects.
26. Failure to cooperate with others in a spirit of harmony.
27. The possession of power or wealth not based on merit or not earned.
28. Lack of the spirit of loyalty to those to whom loyalty is due.
29. Egotism and vanity not under control.
30. Habit of forming opinions and building plans without basing them on first-hand knowledge of the necessary facts.

31. Lack of vision and imagination sufficient to recognize favorable opportunities.

32. Unwillingness to go the extra mile in rendering service.

33. The desire for revenge for real or imaginary injuries by others.

34. The habit of conversing in terms of vulgarity or profanity.

35. The habit of indulging in negative gossip about the affairs of other people.

36. Unsocial attitude toward one's constituted authorities of government.

37. Unbelief in the existence of Infinite Intelligence.

38. Lack of knowlege of how to engage in prayer so as to bring positive results.

39. Failure to benefit by the counsel of others whose experience one often needs.

40. Carelessness in payment of personal debts.

41. The habit of lying or unduly modifying the truth.

42. The habit of offering criticism where it has not been invited.

43. Over-extension in connection with the incurring of indebtedness.

44. Greed for material possessions one does not need.

45. Lack of self-confidence of adequate proportions for the fulfillment of one's chosen objectives.

46. Alcoholism or narcotics.

47. Over-indulgence in smoking, especially the chain-smoking cigarette habit.

48. The habit (of laymen) of serving as their own lawyers in connection with contracts and legal matters.

49. The habit of endorsing other people's notes when the risk is not justified.

50. The habit of procrastination—putting off until tomorrow that which should have been attended to day before yesterday.

51. The habit of running away from unpleasant circumstances instead of mastering them.
52. The habit of talking too much and listening too little. One never learns anything while talking, but always is in the way of learning by listening when others talk.
53. The habit of accepting favors from others without reciprocating.
54. Intentional dishonesty in business and professional relations.

Check yourself carefully by these fifty-four causes of failure, and should the self-examination reveal that you can check O.K. after each of the causes, it is not likely you will ever be overcome by failure. Moreover, if you can check yourself O.K. after each of these causes of failure you need not worry over dental or surgical operations, for you have everything under control.

After you make your own rating, however, it may be both interesting and helpful if you will have some other person rate you on each of these causes of failure— someone who knows you quite well and has the courage to let you look at yourself through his or her eyes.

CHAPTER IX

Sorrow: The Path to the Soul
The Seventh Miracle of Life

SORROW is never invited by individuals, but it is one of the more effective devices of nature through which human beings are conditioned to become humble and cooperative in human relationships.

When a person who has known great sorrow is tempted to criticize or condemn those with whom he may not agree, or those who may have injured him, he often reverses the general rule in such circumstances, and, instead of condemning says: "God pity us all!" When we meet this type of person we intuitively recognize that we are in the presence of royalty!

Sorrow is medicine for the soul, without which the soul would never be recognized by many. Without the leavening influence of sorrow man would still be on the same stem with the animals on the lower plane of intelligence. Sorrow breaks down the barriers which stand between physical man and his spiritual potentialities.

Sorrow breaks up old habits and replaces them with new and better habits—a fact which suggests that sorrow is a device of nature by which she keeps man from becoming enslaved by complacency and self-satisfaction.

Through my one and only great sorrow I discovered the path to my own soul, which gave me freedom I would never have known without this experience, and paved the way for the writing of this book.

Sorrow is closely akin to the emotion of love—the greatest of all the emotions—and during times of disaster sorrow brings people together in a spirit of friendship, and influences man to recognize the blessings of becoming his brother's keeper.

Sorrow softens poverty and embellishes riches!

The riches which are revealed only by sorrow are so great and so varied that inventory of them is impossible. The capacity for sorrow, within itself, is evidence of one's deep spiritual qualities. Knaves never know the emotion of sorrow, for if they knew sorrow they would not be knaves.

Sorrow forces man to take introspective inventory of himself, wherein he may discover the cure for all of his ills and disappointments. And it introduces one to the benefits of meditation and silence, during which unseen forces may bring aid and comfort sufficient unto one's needs at a given time or experience.

When a man comes to himself and discovers the stupendous powers within his command, the revelation usually is of a loved one, failure in business, or some physical affliction beyond his control.

There are certain necessary refinements of body and mind which nature seems to bring about solely by the device of sorrow, such as the elimination of selfishness, arrogance, vanity and self-love.

Sorrow, like failure, may be a blessing or a curse, according to one's reaction to it. If it is accepted as a necessary disciplinary force, without resentment, it may become a great blessing. If it is resented, and one sees no benefits growing out of it, then it may become a curse. The choice is entirely in the mind of the individual.

Sometimes sorrow becomes self-pity, and as such it serves only to weaken the one who so embraces it. Sorrow is beneficial only when it is experienced as an emotional feeling of sympathy for others, or accepted by the individual as a welcome medium of discipline.

One is never in closer contact with Infinite Intelligence than in times of deep sorrow. It is in times of sorrow that prayer is most effective, and often the prayer brings positive results instantly.

Sorrow has revealed to the world geniuses who never would have been recognized except for its deep, soul-searching effects.

Abraham Lincoln's sorrow over the loss of the only woman he ever truly loved, Ann Rutledge, revealed to the world his great soul and gave him to America as our greatest leader in times of our direst need.

Frustration, brought about by unrequited love, often brings one to a turning-point in life at which sorrow makes its appearance, and serves as a guide to great achievements, or a hindrance which may bring total destruction, according to the way the individual relates himself to it.

Here again the choice is entirely with the individual!

Not even the Creator will abrogate one's privilege of controlling his own mind and directing it to whatever ends he may choose, and *no other power can cancel this privilege except by consent of the individual.*

Sorrow may become a mighty power for good when it is transmuted into some sort of constructive action or personal reformation. Sorrow has been known to cure one of the disease of alcoholism after everything else had failed. And it is recognized as a cure for most of the sins of man. Someone has said, "When sorrow fails the Devil takes over."

In times of sorrow people throw off all devices of

pretense and reveal themselves as they are, for sorrow is an hour for open confession of both the humble and the proud. Without the emotion of sorrow man would be an animal as ferocious as the wildest tiger, and infinitely more dangerous because of his superior intelligence.

In lifting man to the highest plane of intelligence, the Creator wisely refined that intelligence with a capacity for sorrow to insure man's moderation in the use of his superiority. Sadists and master criminals usually are individuals of great intelligence who lack the capacity for sorrow.

A man without the capacity for sorrow is the nearest thing to a Devil in the flesh.

If you should ever feel that your sorrows are greater than you can bear, remember you are at the crossroads of life, with four directions from which to choose, one of which may lead you to peace of mind which you would never have found in any other direction, or by any other means. Remember also that the person who has never felt the hand of sorrow has never really lived, for sorrow is the Master-Key to the gateway of one's soul—the port of entrance to Infinite Intelligence.

Sorrow is a stop-gap, a sort of safety valve, which protects those who refuse to heed the guidance of their faculty of reason. Sorrow is a tonic to great souls, a bludgeon to the weak and the undisciplined.

I graduated in the University of Sorrow at the age of fifty. From birth until I reached the age of fifty I had met with about every type of sorrow one can experience, and somehow I had triumphed over all of these. All my rivers of sorrow had been crossed except one, which proved to be the last and the greatest of them all. This was a new sort of sorrow against which I had not built a wall of immunity. It involved the most profound and yet the most dangerous of the emotions—the emotion of love.

I had wandered into the Garden of Love by a path which proved to be a labyrinth over which I found it difficult to back-track. I had seen hundreds of my students make this same mistake and always I had felt something only slightly less than contempt for them because of their weakness. Now the shoe was on the other foot.

At long last I knew the sorrow of unrequited love, and I knew also that I had to find a way to transmute this experience into some form of constructive action. With this experience, as with all previous unpleasant experiences, I began the transmutation by setting for myself a work task which left me no time for regrets.

By some strange move of the Hand of Fate I was guided to the little town of Clinton, South Carolina, where I settled down to overcome my sorrow and rewrite the Science of Success—a task which required over a year. In the apartment where I lived alone was an oil painting of a beautiful forest, through which flowed a wide river that faded from sight at a sharp bend which changed the river's course.

Night after night I sat in front of that painting, waiting and watching for the Ship of Hope to sail around the bend. The ship never came, and the days turned into weeks, the weeks into months, which found me alone with myself. I had always managed to escape from every other unpleasant circumstance of my life, but here I was seemingly inseparably imprisoned with myself, and the boredom seemed greater than I could endure.

I was destined to learn from this experience one of the greatest lessons of my career, namely, that man is not complete without the companionship of the woman of his choice. I could have learned the lesson in no other way.

One evening, after I had been living alone for a year, I was dressing for a dinner engagement and the lights of my apartment were low. I happened to glance at the painting on the wall, and by some strange phenomenon, due to the faint light falling on the picture, I saw a perfect picture of a ship coming around the bend. "My Ship of Hope at last!" I exclaimed.

As I sat across the table from my dinner guest that

evening I made another discovery which clearly revealed to me why I had been guided to the little town of Clinton, for there in front of me sat my future wife—the one for whom I had been searching hither and yon, not knowing that she lived almost next door to me.

So, out of my greatest sorrow, the eternal law of compensation yielded me the greatest of all my riches—a wife perfectly suited in every way to walk arm in arm with me down through the afternoon of life, while we work together putting on the finishing touches of a career through which sorrow has been transmuted into a philosophy destined to benefit millions of people.

But the payoff never would have come, the Science of Success philosophy never would have been organized, had I not learned the blessed art of transmuting unpleasant circumstances into constructive action.

Remember this word "transmute" when you sit in a dentist's chair again, and keep your mind so busily engaged in thinking of something constructive that no time will be left for you to feel physical pain. And when sorrow overtakes you, follow the same plan by turning your thoughts toward the attainment of some as yet unattained purpose; keep it so busy thinking of ways and means of attaining that purpose that no time will be left for self-pity. Do this and you will discover a hidden asset you did not know you possessed—an asset worth more than a king's ransom. *You will discover that you are the master of yourself!*

I know something of the effects of sorrow because I was born in the midst of oceans of it. The home in which I was born was a one-room log cabin located in the mountains of southwest Virginia, and the total assets of that home at the time of my birth consisted of one horse, one cow, one bed and an oven in which my mother baked corn bread.

Theoretically, I had not the ghost of a chance of ever becoming a free man, and less of a chance of ever becoming of service to my fellowmen throughout the world. My parents were poor and they were illiterate. Our neighbors were poor and also illiterate. The only asset of value which I inherited at birth was a sound physical body and a healthy blood stream.

From this brief description of my background you may wonder why I was chosen to give the world its first practical philosophy of personal success. I have often wondered about that myself! But the philosopher tells us that "God moves in a mysterious way His wonders to perform."

Out of the sorrows of my childhood came a passionate desire to lessen the sorrows of others—a desire so strong and enduring that it carried me through more than twenty years of profitless research into the causes of success and failure. Perhaps the sorrows of my youth were sent my way with a purpose, in order that I might be inspired to render the world useful service.

When I say "profitless research" I mean, of course, profitless in monetary compensation while the research was in progress. As to the ultimate compensation which this research yielded me, I can sincerely say I doubt if any other author ever had as much help or as favorable an opportunity to carry on any sort of literary work as I had during those twenty years, while the Science of Success was being organized. At long last those "profitless" years helped me project my influence for good into countless lives, and yielded to me personally more than my share of the Twelve Great Riches *which represent all there is in personal success on this earthly plane.*

If I could go back and live my life over again, would I avoid those sorrows of my youth? No, definitely I would not, for it was those experiences which tempered my body and mind and refined my soul for a task in life which has resulted to the benefit of others who are struggling to find their way through the Black Forest of the Jungle of Life.

Get the full significance of the thought I am here trying

to convey, and you will understand why I stated that this volume would be something profoundly greater than the mere instructions on how to master the fear of dentistry or surgical operations. If I do my work as I have hoped I might do it, in writing this volume, *it will introduce the reader to a source of power with which all unpleasant circumstances can be transmuted into helpful service*—a source of power which operates through that "other self" which one does not see when looking into a mirror.

Once you learn to properly evaluate sorrow you will recognize its benefits whenever they appear, and you will understand it is one of the more essential devices of nature *with which she separates man from his animalistic background*. Animals on all planes of development lower than that of man, never feel the beneficent emotion of sorrow, with the exception of the dog whose long partnership with man has made the dog something closely akin to, but slightly less than, a human being.

If you have a great capacity for sorrow you have also a great potential capacity for genius, provided you relate yourself to sorrow as a welcome source of discipline and not as a medium of self-pity.

As we continue on our trip through the Valley of the Great Miracles, you will observe that each of them is definitely embellished with spiritual potentialities of great benefit to those who correctly interpret them. And you will observe also *that peace of mind is available only to those who properly interpret and relate themselves to the laws of nature.* If you miss this point you will have missed the major purpose which prompted the writing of this book!

Sorrow is the great universal denominator which serves to compose the circumstances of a community, or a family, when misfortune strikes. I have known sorrow to bring together estranged husbands and wives who would have yielded to no other influence, and I have seen sorrow wipe out mountain feuds which had existed for generations.

The emotion of sorrow, like the emotion of love, refines the souls of those who experience it, and gives them courage and faith to meet the trials and tribulations of struggle in a world of confusion and chaos, *provided always that sorrow is accepted as a benefit and not as a curse.* Resentment of sorrow develops stomach ulcers, high blood pressure and general unfriendliness from other people.

Every sorrow brings with it the seed of an equivalent joy! Look for that seed, germinate it and reap the benefit of the joy. When you can do this, you will no longer permit yourself to be annoyed by so trivial a matter as *dental or surgical operations, even if they are major operations.* Instead of coddling yourself when you meet with sorrow, look around until you find someone with a greater sorrow than yours, and help him or her to master it. And lo, *your own sorrow will have been transmuted into medicine for your body and your soul*—the sort of medicine with which you may cure many other types of unpleasant experiences.

CHAPTER X

Nature's Definiteness of Purpose
The Eighth Miracle of Life

FIXATION OF NATURAL LAWS is a miracle which forever safeguards all of nature's plans and purposes, and insures that the overall plan of the universe will be carried out *without the possibility of interference from man.*

The Law of Cosmic Habitforce is the comptroller of all other natural laws, and is the power which gives fixation to all habits of every living thing in the lower orders of life than that of man. It also fixes the habits of energy and matter as well as the distances and the relationships between all the stars and planets.

Man alone has been provided with the privilege and the means by which he may fix his own habits, good or bad. The habits of all living things, on a lower plane of life, have been fixed by what we call "instinct," and the instinct pattern of each living thing on this lower plane represents the limitations and full extent of its activities.

Man's privilege to make and to break his own habits has been so definitely left in his own hands that he is not bound by any form of inherited limitations, such as are all lower forms of life. That great universal truth, "Whatever the mind of man can conceive and believe, the mind can achieve," is given sound foundation because of man's power to break all habits which have been fastened upon him by the Law of Cosmic Habitforce, and supplement them with other habits of his own choosing.

Once a man chooses a goal and creates plans for attaining it, Cosmic Habitforce will fix all his habits which are related to that goal so that they automatically lead him in the direction of the goal. However, man can break those habits at will, change his plans and his objectives, and set up an entirely new set of habits for the attainment of his objective.

This power of choice in the selection and control of habits gives man a rating *but one step below that of Infinite Intelligence,* and, in fact, gives him the privilege of drawing upon the forces of Infinite Intelligence at will for the attainment of all his aims and purposes. For evidence to support this observation one has only to take inventory of man's achievements during the first half of the twentieth century, during which man revealed more of nature's carefully hidden secrets than had been uncovered during the entire previous existence of mankind.

Step by step, by the exercise of his self-established habits of thought, man was ushered in the push-button age which permits him, figuratively speaking, to supply his every need by calmly sitting down and pushing buttons which set up vibrations in whatever direction he may desire.

Perhaps this evolutionary advancement of man, through which he has transferred to machines most of the labors he previously performed by hand, is only a part of nature's plan of introducing man to his own mind-power by the process of elimination. When there is no longer any need for the use of physical power, man will then have time to discover and use his brain power; and in that discovery he may learn that he can do all the things which the Nazarene challenged him to do—*"Even greater things than I have done."*

The stars and planets, and the nebulous matter from which these were formed, are related to one another by nature's habits of fixation, operating through the Law of Cosmic Habitforce. Day and night, the seasons of the year, the law of balance, and every living thing except man, are bound by inexorable habits which make their movements and actions accurately predictable over long periods of time and far in advance of the happenings.

Man alone has been given the privilege of fixing his own earthly destiny, with the right to make it pleasant or unpleasant, successful, or unsuccessful, happy or unhappy, rich or poor, and his achievements are always unpredictable because his potential power is unlimited.

If man had but two more privileges than he now possesses he would be on an equal footing with the Creator; namely, (1) the privilege of coming into the world at birth, of his own choice; and (2) the privilege of remaining among the living as long as he desires. Man has potential control over almost everything else, but alas, he rarely discovers the powers available to him or makes any attempt to use these powers for his own uplift, or to make this a better world.

For the most part, man settles down in a sort of tug-of-war struggle with forces which become unfriendly toward him because he does not understand them—forces such as the great miracles of life—and he gladly settles with life for a place to sleep, a little food to fill his belly and enough clothes to hide his nakedness.

Once in a long while an individual steps out of the long procession of human beings, takes possession of his own mind, recognizes its powers and makes use of them. Then the world has found an Edison, or a Ford, or a Luther Burbank, or an Alexander Graham Bell, or a Henry J. Kaiser—men who have removed all self-imposed limitations because they learned the truth that "Whatever the mind can conceive and believe, the mind can achieve."

Geniuses? Yes, because genius is simply a matter of self-discovery!

Know yourself—your "other self" which does not recognize limitations—and you may become "the Master of Your Fate, the Captain of Your Soul," and peace of mind will come to you as naturally as the eating of a meal when you are hungry.

Man's major weakness consists not in riches he does not possess, but in the *failure to make use of that which he has!* In every generation of people, less than one percent of those who are living take over the torchlight of civilization and carry it over for the benefit of the next generation. Civilization is kept on the march by those who discover and make use of their own minds. The same is true in the average business enterprise, where a relatively small percentage of the individuals connected with the business are responsible for its successful operation. *The others are there in body but not in mind and spirit,* and often they take out of the business more than they contribute to it.

Nature does not vacillate; does not procrastinate; does not change her plans, and in this respect she sets a beautiful example for people to follow. The successful ones do follow the example; *the failures do not.*

One of the impressive discoveries revealed to me during my contact with the successful men and women who helped me organize the Science of Success, consisted in the fact that they moved with definiteness of purpose, and never wavered, slowed down, or quit when the going was hard. They succeeded because they knew what they desired, laid plans for attaining it, and followed those plans until they were rewarded with success.

I have often thought, when observing successful people who stick to their purpose through failure after failure, *that Infinite Intelligence throws itself on the side of the person who will not quit when obstacles have to be sur-*

mounted; for somehow these people always triumph eventually, no matter how many handicaps they have to master.

When I first heard that Thomas A. Edison had surmounted more than ten thousand failures before he found the secret of the incandescent electric lamp, I wondered how any human being could or would pay such a high price for victory. Later, after I became intimately acquainted with the Edison mind, and the method with which he applied it to the solution of his problems, *I discovered that it was the disciplinary effects of those ten thousand failures which made Edison the greatest inventor of all times.*

Edison must have recognized, as he met with one failure after another, that persistence would eventually bring him the secret he was seeking. I am led to this conclusion because of my own experiences in times of failure, when I was searching for the causes of success and failure, for each failure with which I met had only the effect of making me more determined to keep on until I met with success. That small, still voice which speaks to one from within kept telling me not to quit when I was overtaken by defeat.

If we could only experience, for a single time, the hurts of both the physical and mental pains felt by those who go through the period of struggle before they meet with victory in the upper brackets of human achievements, we would be utterly ashamed to admit the fear of so trivial an experience as that of dental surgery or major operations.

CHAPTER XI

Nature's Profound Bookkeeping System
The Ninth Miracle of Life

NATURE'S UNIVERSAL BALANCE is another device by which nature maintains a perfect balance of everything that exists throughout the universe, including: (1) Time, (2) Space, (3) Energy, (4) Matter, and (5) Intelligence, through which these known factors are shaped into every specialized form known to man.

Through the operation of this automatic law, nature has made it compulsory that every individual person be forced to taste both the bitter and the sweet experiences of life, but she has wisely and cleverly injected into this law a compensating agency which aids the individual in balancing the bitter and the sweet according to his own needs and desires. This provision was necessary because the Creator's overall plan provides that man shall have unquestioned control over his own mind, with the privilege of directing it to either bitter or sweet ends.

Through the operation of this compensating device, which is a portion of the great law of Universal Balance, every adversity, every defeat, every failure, every disappointment, every human frustration of whatsoever nature or cause, brings with it, in the circumstance itself, the seed of an equivalent benefit. This fact cannot be emphasized too strongly; hence the repetition.

Under the provisions of this compensating device, every person has the right and the power to find that seed of an equivalent benefit in every undesirable or unpleasant experience which may overtake him, whether the experience is of his own making or beyond his control, and germinate the seed into the full-blown flower, then the ripened fruit of some desirable thing which will compensate him for the adversity which yielded the seed.

Here we find evidence in abundance of the Infinite Justice with which all individuals are related to themselves and to one another. Nature has so designed the overall laws of the universe that injustice is impossible for those who learn to interpret her laws and to live by them. Injustice is purely a man-made institution which exists nowhere except in man's relationship with his fellowmen. In man's relationship with the natural laws of the universe there can be no injustice, because those laws have cleverly provided the method by which man *automatically punishes himself for his misdeeds, and he may compensate himself for his virtues,* by correctly interpreting nature's laws and harmoniously adapting himself to them.

There are two kinds of circumstances which affect the lives of people:

(1) Circumstances which do not originate as the result of something the individual does or neglects to do, and therefore are not subject to control by the individual. Such circumstances, for instance, as the death of loved ones, birth with physical afflictions of such a nature that the affliction cannot be corrected, or birth in under-privileged racial classes.

(2) Circumstances over which the individual has the privilege of control and the power with which to exercise that privilege, such, for example, as fear, greed, jealousy,

vanity, egotism, lust, hatred, envy, ill health, poverty, controversies with relatives, neighbors or business associates, antagonism with others over politics, religion and personal views. This list could be extended to cover practically every human relationship but in final analysis it covers circumstances affecting one's life over which the individual has the means of control, despite the fact that *he may seldom exercise that control.*

Circumstances in group one, which are not under the individual's control, can be blocked off from influencing the individual's peace of mind by the mere exercise of the Great Prerogative provided by the Creator, whereby every individual has the power to establish and control his own *mental atttitude* and direct his power of thought to any desired end, *including the absolute control of his reaction to all experiences of his life.* In other words, circumstances which cannot be controlled can be eliminated from the influence of one's mental attitude in such a way that they do not exist, and the individual may conduct himself precisely the same as if they did not exist. This is a hard task, someone may complain. Yes, it is, but the means by which it may be made easy will be disclosed later on during our trip through the Valley of Miracles.

Circumstances in group two, those which are under the control of the individual, can be disposed of through the aid of the most important and powerful of all the Great Miracles.

This Universal Balancing Law extends not only to human beings in all their problems and relationships with one another, but also to trees and all things which grow from the soil of the earth. Observe, for example, the perfect engineering and symmetrical balancing of a tree, with its branches draped to keep the tree in balance on all sides, the roots in proportion to the body and the branches of the tree, and imbedded in the ground to the proper depth—*a job of engineering no man could duplicate.*

Universal Balancing extends also to all inanimate matter, down to the smallest units of matter—the electrons and protons of the atom which are held in perfect balance by two equal units of power—one negative unit and one positive unit—so balanced through a sort of tug-of-war that one pulls and the other pushes to a point of stalemate which creates the balance.

Throughout that portion of *our universe* which we have been able to explore we find a perfect system of balancing between all the stars and planets, and the nebulous matter which has not yet taken on the form of planets or stars. If this Law of Balance did not exist there would be constant chaos through the collisions of the stars and planets, and the seasons of the year, and day and night, would not be regulated or their habits predictable.

Most of us may not feel a deep interest in the balancing of the stars and planets, but all of us do have a keen interest in the methods by which we may take full advantage of the great Law of Universal Balance in adjusting the circumstances affecting our individual lives so that they benefit us. The best way to secure benefits from this great law is, first, by taking possession of our power of thought and using it to relate ourselves to the circumstances we can control, in a manner favorable to ourselves; and second, to use this same power of thought to adjust ourselves beneficially to all the circumstances affecting our lives which we cannot control.

From this brief analysis of the Law of Balance we are heartened and encouraged by the observation that this law keeps everything throughout the universe in line with nature's established pattern and plan, except man—the only living creature with the power to deviate from the influence of this, and all other natural laws, if and when he chooses, *and is willing to pay the price for his deviation.*

If you are searching for the supreme secret of success in all human endeavors, here is a very suitable point at which to stop, ponder, meditate and think, with the hope that the small still voice which speaks from within may bless you with the knowledge you seek.

CHAPTER XII

Time: Nature's Universal Cure for All Ills
The Tenth Miracle of Life

TIME is the great Universal Doctor of human ills, whose chief agent is the ether, the energy which connects everything with every other thing in the universe. TIME is the great healer of wounds, both physical and mental, and it is the transformer of all *causes* into their *appropriate effects*.

TIME trades irrational youth for maturity of age and wisdom!

TIME transmutes the wounds of the heart and the frustrations of our daily lives into courage, endurance and understanding. Without this kindly and beneficent service most individuals would be lost in the early days of their youth.

TIME ripens the grain in the fields and the fruit of the trees and makes them ready for human enjoyment and sustenance.

TIME gives hotheads a chance to cool off and become rational.

TIME helps us discover the great laws of nature, by the

trial and error method, and helps us profit by our mistakes of judgment.

TIME is our most precious possession, because we can be sure of no more than a single second of it on any given date or place.

TIME is the agent of mercy through which we may repent of our sins and errors and gain useful knowledge therefrom.

TIME favors those who interpret nature's laws correctly and who adapt them as guideposts to the correct habits of living, but Time swings heavily with penalties for those who ignore or neglect her laws.

TIME is the master manipulator of the universal law of Cosmic Habitforce, the fixer of all habits, both of living creatures and inanimate things. Time is also the master manipulator of the lesser law of compensation, through the operation of which everyone reaps that which he sows. (The positive operation of this law is called the law of increasing returns; the negative operation is called the law of diminishing returns.)

TIME does not always operate the law of compensation swiftly, but it does operate definitely, according to fixed habits and patterns which the philosopher understands, and by which he can foretell the nature of coming events by examining the *cause* from which they are to spring.

TIME is also the master manipulator of the great Law of Change which keeps all things and all people in a constant state of flux, and never allows them to remain the same for two minutes in succession. This truth is laden with benefits of stupendous proportions because it provides the means by which we may correct our mistakes, eliminate our false fears and weak habits, and exchange ignorance for wisdom and peace of mind as we grow older.

Go back into your past experiences and take count of the occasions when your troubled heart found no surcease from its aches save only by the merciful hand of Doctor Time.

If you have failed in business or in some occupational undertaking which you chose as your life work, you may have observed that TIME came to your rescue with other and perhaps greater opportunities; and you rejoiced that you had been detoured from your course to a smoother and broader highway of opportunity.

On the next occasion when you find yourself wasting a single second of this precious agent of OPPORTUNITY, TIME, copy the following resolution, commit it to memory, and start immediately to carry it out:

My Commitment to Doctor Time:

1. Time is my greatest asset, and I shall relate myself to it on a budget system which provides that every second not devoted to sleep shall be used for self-improvement.

2. In the future I shall regard the loss, through neglect, of any portion of my Time as a sin, for which I must atone by the better use in the future of an equivalent amount of it.

3. Recognizing that I shall reap that which I sow, I shall sow only the seeds of service which may benefit others as well as myself, and thereby throw myself in the way of the great Law of Compensation.

4. I shall so use my Time in the future that each day will bring me some measure of peace of mind, in the absence of which I shall recognize that the seed I have been sowing needs reexamination.

5. Knowing that my habits of thought become the patterns which attract all the circumstances affecting my life through the lapse of Time, I shall keep my mind so busy in connection with the circumstances I *desire* that no Time will be left to devote to fears and frustrations, and the things *I do not desire*.

6. Recognizing that, at best, my allotted Time on the earth plane is indefinite and limited, I shall endeavor

in all ways possible to use my portion of it so that those nearest me will benefit by my influence, and be inspired by my example to make the best possible use of their own Time.

7. Finally, when my allotment of Time shall have expired, I hope I may leave behind me a monument to my name—not a monument in stone, but in the hearts of my fellowmen—a monument whose marking will testify that the world was made a little better because of my having passed this way.

8. I shall repeat this Commitment daily during the remainder of my allotment of Time, and back it with BELIEF that it will improve my character and inspire those whom I may influence, to likewise improve their lives.

The hands of the Clock of Time are moving swiftly onward! We cry out, "Backward, turn backward O Time in your flight," but Time does not heed your cries.

It is later than you think!

Arouse yourself, fellow wayfarer; awake and take possession of your own mind while you still have enough Time to become, during the yet unexpired future, that which you would have liked to have been in the past.

Make the most of your present allotment of Time, with the hope that you will not have to reincarnate in order to do the job all over again because of neglect.

You have been warned!

Now the responsibility is YOURS. There is a simple test by which you may judge whether or not you have been using your Time to best advantage. If you have attained peace of mind and material opulence sufficient for your needs, your Time has been properly used. If you have not attained these blessings, your Time has not been properly used, and you should begin now to search for the circumstances in connection with which you have fallen short.

The truly great people have no such reality as "idle time," because they keep their minds geared eternally to patterns of constructive thought. By this profound use of their Time, they develop an alert sixth sense through which they look, listen, and see from within.

If negative thoughts stray into the minds of the truly great, these thoughts are immediately transmuted into positive thoughts and exercised by positive physical action appropriate to their nature.

Tick, tick, tick—the pendulum of the Clock of Time is swinging rapidly!

The entire face of civilization is undergoing an uplifting operation.

Mr. Right and Mr. Wrong are engaged in mortal combat for supremacy. The Time has come for everyone to stand up and be counted. The use each of us makes of his individual allotment of Time will tell whose side each of us is on—Mr. Right's or Mr. Wrong's.

Something has speeded up the Clock of Time so rapidly that the last half of the twentieth century will reveal to mankind more individual opportunities for self-improvement than have been revealed during the entire past of man's existence.

Your share of these vast OPPORTUNITIES may be embraced and used only by the way you relate yourself to TIME!

CHAPTER XIII

The American Way of Life Makes Men Free
The Eleventh Miracle of Life

FREEDOM OF THE AMERICAN WAY OF LIFE is one of the Great Miracles of all times. Here in the United States of America the stage has been set and the way has been prepared, as nowhere else on this earth at any period of time, for man to take full and complete possession of his own mind and direct it to whatever ends he may desire.

Our American Way of Life was born by the shedding of tears of blood, and matured through hardship and struggle which touched the lives of every living citizen of the nation; all of which indicates that our way of life harmonizes in every particular with the Creator's plan to allow all men to become free by the exercise of their own minds.

Evidence that ours is a land of OPPORTUNITY, where every person may choose his own objective in life and achieve it, through the operation of his own mind, is available in overwhelming abundance. Where else on earth, except in America, could an uneducated Italian immigrant, such as A. B. Giannina, start his career by pushing a banana cart and pyramid his efforts into the ownership of the world's largest banking system—the Bank of America?

Where else but in America could a young, uneducated mechanic give birth to an industry like that of the automobile industry, and without capital to begin with, pyramid his humble beginning into a world-wide empire with a fabulous fortune, and provide employment for hundreds of thousands of people, as did Henry Ford?

And where, except in the United States, does the humblest laborer enjoy more of the modern conveniences of living than did kings and potentates a few generations ago?

Where else on earth, except in the United States, is every citizen provided with adequate motives of self-aggrandizement sufficient to inspire him to act on his own personal initiative, choose his own career, think his own thoughts, and express them in any manner he may choose?

Where else is every male child born as a potential holder of the highest office the people have to offer, and where else has such a high office been successfully administered by a humble rail-splitter?

Where, except in the United States of America, can any individual of any race or creed walk with dignity upon the earth and say truly, "I am free?"

Where, except in America, could an uneducated lad choose as his career the business of inventing, surround himself with a Master Mind of scientifically skilled men, and make himself one of the greatest inventors of all times, as did Thomas A. Edison?

I have posed these questions for you, who enjoy the largess of the great American Way of Life, with the hope that you who read this volume will answer them, each in his own way, according to the benefits this country may have provided him; and in searching your hearts and minds for the answers, learn to better evaluate the vast opportunities open to *you* in any calling you may choose.

Before we leave this analysis of the Great American Way of Life let us be reminded that this heritage will remain ours only so long as we recognize it, use it properly and protect it. Like all other blessings conferred upon man by Mother Nature, our rights to the privileges we enjoy in America will remain only as long as we earn the right to them. Nature looks with great disfavor on the idea of *something for nothing.*

CHAPTER XIV

Wisdom Robs Death of Its Sting
The Twelfth Miracle of Life

THE MYSTERY OF DEATH: It may be difficult for most people to interpret Death as being anything but an unavoidable tragedy, but this limited view of the subject can be broadened by taking account of the overall plan of the universe, which is in a constant state of flux, constantly undergoing *eternal change*.

Man comes to the earth plane without his knowledge or consent, remains in the Great School of Life a little while, then passes into another plane of intelligence without his consent. It is not a part of the Creator's plan for man to live on the earth plane forever, and it would be tragedy if it were a part of the overall plan.

Could anyone think of anything more frightful than to be compelled to remain forever on this earth plane of struggle, where life itself depends upon eternal vigilance on the part of the individual?

The life span is something like the modern school system. We enter the kindergarten period, graduate from there into the grades, then into high school, and from there we enter the last stage by entering college. The major purpose behind man's brief interlude on earth seems to be that of education.

If there had been no device of Death, think of the evil men the world has known—men who would still be living and making life miserable for everyone—the would-be conquerors and self-appointed dictators who have sought, from the dawn of civilization, to enslave all mankind.

Death is but an extended form of sleep, during which the individual sheds his tired, worn out physical body for one that is inexhaustible and eternal. Therefore it is a circumstance over which the individual has no final control, and it should be accepted as such and dismissed from the mind.

Understand the Law of Change, which is a part of the universal system, and Death becomes understandable, and may readily be accepted as a necessity. There could not coexist in the universe an eternal Law of Change and eternal life on the earth plane.

The individual may fear death, dread to meet with it, and look upon it as a tragedy, but fortunately the individual is only a pawn in relation to the overall plan of the universe, and as such his desires and the means of their fulfillment are confined entirely to that brief interlude known as Life, over which the individual has been given a free hand, to spend his brief visit in whatever manner he pleases.

The attitude of the philosopher toward Death seems to be the sensible one. He accepts it as a circumstance over which he has but a slight, limited control; therefore, he adjusts himself to it in a neutral spirit of belief that when it comes he will be ready for it, and he then dismisses the subject and devotes his energies to making his life yield all the benefits he can *in connection with those circumstances over which he has control.*

The philosopher looks upon those who fear Death as offering insult to their Creator. And the philosopher accepts every circumstance which touches his life as grist for the Mill of Life, and promptly adjusts himself to all such circumstances in a manner best suited to enable him to benefit from them.

Some of the Great Miracles constitute the major impedimenta standing in the way of peace of mind of the majority of people. The purpose of this analysis of the Miracles of Life is to help the individual relate himself to them in a mental attitude which will change them from things to be dreaded, to circumstances which can be made beneficial to his interests.

Through this analysis of the Great Miracles, the "Worry Bird" (which most people feed unnecessarily) has been robbed of the food necessary to keep it alive, and the way has been cleared for peace of mind, based on the acceptance of all the circumstances of life, just as they are.

It is my hope that each of you who read this volume will be conditioned, upon finishing this chapter, to properly interpret and apply the principles set forth in subsequent chapters, which have been designed to help you relate yourself to the Miracles in a manner that will give you the greatest benefits.

When this hope shall have been realized, then you will have found peace of mind which will endure throughout the remainder of your life.

The statements I have made in this analysis are not important. *But the thinking on your part, which the statements may have inspired, is important!* For it may well be that the thinking thus inspired may give you a change of attitude toward Life which will make Life sweeter as the years grow fewer.

CHAPTER XV

The Limitless Power of the Mind
The Thirteenth Miracle of Life

THE MIND OF MAN would lead all the other Miracles of Life if they had been described in the order of their importance, because the mind is the instrument through which man relates himself to all things and circumstances that affect or influence his life.

Without doubt the human mind is the most mysterious, the most awe-inspiring product which nature has produced, and at the same time it is the least understood, and the most often abused, of man's profound gifts from the Creator.

The mind is the citadel of the soul, wherein is housed the connecting link between the conscious thinking process of man and Infinite Intelligence. It is the switchboard, so to speak, through which man may tune in and communicate directly with the great universal reservoir of Infinite Intelligence, and draw therefrom the answers to all his problems, the way of fulfillment of all his hopes, dreams, and aspirations.

And most profound of all, *the mind is the one and only*

thing over which the Creator has given man the complete right of control; a prerogative which not even the Creator has set aside, reversed, or in any manner usurped, which strongly suggests that the mind was intended for man's exclusive use; that it is the most important of all the gifts of the Creator; and the means by which man may control the major portion of his earthly destiny.

All of man's successes and all of his failures and frustrations are the direct result of the manner in which he used his mind, *or neglects to use it.*

The functional operations of the mind are divided into nine departments, something on the order of a well-organized business. Some of these departments function automatically, without direction by the individual, while other departments *are under the control of the individual at all times.*

Here is a breakdown of all the departments of the mind:

(a) THE FACULTY OF WILL: The Will is the "big boss" of all the other departments of the mind. Here is the starting point where the individual begins to exercise his Great Prerogative privilege of *exclusive control over his thoughts.* The faculty of the Will is the "yes" and the "no" man of the entire mind. It carries out orders of the individual, regardless of their nature or the effect they may have upon the individual. The power of the Will remains strong in exact proportion to its use. An idle Will, like an idle arm, will become soft and weak.

(b) THE FACULTY OF REASON: The faculty of Reason is the "presiding judge" of the mind. When directed, or permitted, to do so, it will pass judgment on all ideas, aims, desires, purposes, and circumstances which the individual brings to its attention; but its decisions can be set aside by the "big boss," the Will, or offset by the influence of the emotions if the Will does not assert itself. One of the major weaknesses of all so-called thinking is the tendency of individuals to allow their Wills to be set aside by their emotions. This error can be, and it often is, tragic, because the emotions have no relation to logic or reason; therefore, all action growing out of the emotions should have careful attention of the Will.

(c) THE FACULTY OF EMOTIONS: Here is the starting place of a major portion of all actions of the mind. People make decisions which harmonize with their "feelings," and engage in activities which have not been previewed by the faculties of Reason and Will. Such decisions are more often unsound than sound.

The most common reckless use of the emotions, without due attention from the faculties of Reason and Will, originates through the emotion of Love. The emotion of Love partakes of a spiritual quality of the highest order, but it may be, and it often is, the most dangerous of all the emotions because people generally do not submit it to the modifying influence of the Reason and the Will.

Accurate thinkers—people who use all the departments of their minds in the process of thinking—never allow the emotion of Love to express itself until its actions have been carefully looked over by the Reason and the Will. Moreover, the accurate thinker submits all of his deepest desires, plans, and purposes to his departments of Reason and Will *to make sure that his eagerness and enthusiasm do not overthrow his Wisdom;* and his emotion of Love is always under constant suspicion lest it get from under his control.

(d) THE FACULTY OF IMAGINATION: This faculty is the architect of man's soul through which he may pattern his own earthly destiny to suit himself and change or modify that pattern as often as he pleases. With the aid of his Imagination, man may penetrate the interstellar spaces of infinitude with the speed of lightning, conquer the air above him and the seas below him, and create a million ideas and concepts of benefit to himself by merely combining in new ways old ideas and concepts.

Through his Imagination man may combine fantasy with realism and shape these into living empires of industry which change the entire trend of civilization. Nothing is impossible of accomplishment by the Imagination which is guided by the faculties of Will and Reason, but *unbridled Imagination can play havoc with an individual's life;* and it has been said that when the emotion of Love and the Imagination get together and go on an unchaperoned spree, the individual may never recover from the damage they do.

The Imagination is the place of origin of the sixty-four dollar physical ailment know as hypochondria, which has proved to be a major problem with doctors. It may also be the place of origin of the cure for hypochondria, and there are many reliable authorities who claim that the Imagination exercises such powerful influence over the physical body that it can activate the body resistance mechanism and cause it to eliminate many types of real physical ailments.

The Imagination is a great institution whose *potentialities are practically unlimited, but it is a very tricky institution which requires constant supervision by the faculties of the Reason and the Will*. It may be helpful if you will read the preceding sentence many times, until you become impressed by the potency of the suggestion it carries.

(e) THE FACULTY OF CONSCIENCE: Here we have the department of the mind which gives moral guidance to the individual. If allowed to function without interference, the Conscience carefully processes all of the individual's aims and purposes and warns him when they do not harmonize with the moral laws of nature. This warning ceases and the Conscience eventually goes out of business altogether *if the individual fails or neglects to heed its warnings*.

The individual who has the full support of his Conscience in connectioin with all his desires, aims and purposes, has direct access to the necessary Faith to enable him to accomplish whatever he may set his heart and mind upon.

(f) THE FIVE PHYSICAL SENSES: The five senses —sight, sound, taste, smell and touch—are the physical "arms" of the brain, through which it contacts the external world and acquires information. The senses are not always reliable, therefore, they require constant supervision by the faculty of Reason and the Will.

Under any sort of highly emotional activity, the senses often become confused and highly undependable, as in the case of sudden fright, or intense anger. No decision which is reached under the influence of fear or anger should be allowed to stand, until it has been thoroughly reviewed by Will and Reason.

(g) THE FACULTY OF MEMORY: Here is the "filing cabinet" of the brain wherein is stored all thought impulses, all conscious experiences, and all sensations which reach the brain through the five physical senses. The Memory is also very undependable, as most individuals can testify. Therefore, it needs supervision and discipline by the Will and the Reason. The main cause for the unreliability of the Memory is due to the fact that the "filing clerk"—the individual who supervises the action of the Memory—is careless in not having a definite system by which to work.

The Memory can be made reasonably reliable with the aid of a practical Memory training course, such as the Roth system. Reliability of the Memory is entirely a matter of discipline, supervision, and education of the "filing clerk" who is responsible for the function of this important faculty of the mind.

(h) THE "SIXTH SENSE": This is the broadcasting and the receiving station of the mind through which one automatically sends and receives vibrations of thought, and perhaps other still higher vibrations which emanate on planes of intelligence outside that of our own earth. This is the medium of communication between the individual and the Unseen Guides which are believed to be available for his service.

The "Sixth Sense" is the medium through which a properly qualified mind may communicate with other minds, at any distance, through the principle of telepathy. The principle of telepathy has been recognized, by reliable authorities, as a workable reality, and the means by which it may be put into service has been described in detail in many books, including some which I have written.

(i) THE SUBCONSCIOUS SECTION OF THE MIND: This is the "switchboard" through which the conscious section of the mind may communicate directly with infinite Intelligence. The Subconscious acts upon any idea, plan, or purpose which reaches it, and it makes no attempt to distinguish the difference between positive and negative, or right or wrong influences. But it does respond more quickly and effectively to influences which have been highly emotionalized with such emotions as fear, anger, *belief,* and *faith.*

The Subconscious section of the mind is amenable to the influences of the conscious section of the mind, which often stubbornly closes the door to the Subconscious through fears and limitations and false beliefs. In order to get around these negative barricades set up by the conscious section of the mind, and in order to give directions to the Subconscious for the cure of physical ailments, doctors of Suggestive Therapeutics often wait until the individual is asleep (sometimes through hypnotism) and then communicate directly with the Subconscious.

As stated earlier, there is a machine in successful operation with which any desired order can be given to the Subconscious while the individual is asleep. The orders or instructions are recorded on a phonograph record and placed on the machine which plays them every fifteen minutes (until the individual awakes and turns off the machine). The machine is operated by a clock which can be set to start the playing of the record after the individual is asleep.

The references in this volume to the departments of

the mind are, of necessity, brief and not intended as exhaustive analyses of these subjects, but merely a bird's-eye picture of the "mechanism" through which the human mind operates, together with a brief description of the extent to which the departments of the mind are under the control of the individual.

We would emphasize that all thought, whether it is negative or positive, sound or unsound, tends to clothe itself in its physical equivalent, and it proceeds to do so by inspiring the individual with ideas, plans, and purposes for the attainment of desired ends, through natural and logical means. After thought on any subject becomes, through repetition, a habit, it is taken over and automatically acted upon by the Subconscious.

It may not be true that "thoughts are things," but it is true that thoughts create things, and the things thus created are strikingly similar to the nature of the thoughts from which they are fashioned.

It is believed by many people, who are competent to judge accurately, that every thought which one releases starts an unending vibration with which the one who releases it will have to contend later; that man himself is but the physical reflection of thought put into motion by Infinite Intelligence. It is also the belief of many that the energy with which people think is but a projected portion of Infinite Intelligence which the individual appropriates from the universal source, through the equipment of the brain.

We have now reached the point at which we shall begin the explanation of the means by which one's mind may be conditioned for dentistry, major surgical operations, or any other unpleasant experience which one may have to face.

The *conditioning* of the mind must be done entirely through the subconscious section of the mind. Therefore, let us have a further look at the means by which the subconscious may be reached and directed to any desired end at will.

You cannot *entirely control* your subconscious mind, but you can voluntarily influence it to act upon any desire, plan, or purpose which you may wish translated into concrete form.

The subconscious never remains idle. If you neglect to keep it busy with desires of your own choice it will feed upon the thoughts inspired by your environment, especially those associated with the things you do not want, the things you fear or dislike.

Whether you recognize it or not, you are living daily in the midst of all sorts of thought impulses which are reaching your subconscious mind without your knowledge. Some of these impulses are negative; some are positive. You are now about to be informed how to shut off the flow of negative influences which reach and influence you, and the means by which these negative influences, including all fears, may be supplanted by desires, plans, and purposes *of your own choosing,* including, in particular, the means of mastering physical pain.

When you master the technique you are about to receive, and learn to apply it, you will possess the key which unlocks the door to your subconscious mind, *and you will control that door so completely that no undesirable thoughts or influences can pass through it.*

Before we describe the method of approach to the subconscious mind you should recognize that there are two doors to your subconscious. One door opens outward toward the physical world in which you live, and that world can be entered only through that door. *The other door opens inwardly and connects directly with the great universal reservoir of Infinite Intelligence.*

It is through these two doors that prayer operates.

It is through these two doors that one's hopes, desires, and plans may be fulfilled through *definiteness of purpose* and a *burning desire* for its realization.

It is through these two doors that all of one's fears, doubts, and discouragements are translated into the miseries of life *if the conscious mind is allowed to dwell upon these undesirable conditions.* Every thought one sends to the subconscious mind; every thought which reaches the subconscious mind because of one's neglect to process and reject negative thoughts inspired by one's environment, is automatically accepted by the subconscious and acted upon.

One of the greatest of the inconsistencies of mankind is the fact that the majority of people go through life with their minds devoted largely to thinking of all the things and circumstances *they do not wish*—poverty, failure, ill health, unhappiness, and physical pain—and they then wonder why they are cursed with all of these undesirable conditions.

The mind attracts to one the exact material equivalent of that which one thinks about most often. Along with this statement of fact, remember that the Creator provided every normal person with complete, unchallengeable right and power to control and direct his mind power to whatever ends he may choose, and you will have no difficulty in recognizing that *all undesirable circumstances one meets with are the results of neglect to take possession of the mind and to guide it to the ends one desires.*

Hypochondria, The Doctor's $64.00 Word

Hypochondria means *imaginary* physical ailment! It is a conservative statement to say that this ailment gives doctors and dentists more trouble than all the real ailments known to mankind. The fear of ill health, and its first cousin, the fear of physical pain, are inherited states of mind, and they constitute one of the Seven Basic Fears with which all people suffer at one time or another.

In my public lectures some years ago, I gave dramatic demonstrations of the nature of this inborn fear of ill health, and of physical pain—demonstrations which proved that persons with not a single trace of physical ailments could be made violently ill by mere suggestion.

The technique by which this was demonstrated was very simple. With the aid of four assistants, who were stationed secretly at various places in and out of the auditorium where I was lecturing, the demonstration was carried out. A "victim" was secretly chosen from the audience by a committee of my students. At recess, by prearrangement with my "stooges," each of them approached the "victim" and asked him or her questions.

Stooge number one would ask, "Are you not feeling well? You look as if you are ill." Stooge number two would rush up to the "victim" and in an excited voice exclaim, "I say, my friend, you look as if you are about to faint! Can I get you a drink of water?" Stooge number three would soon appear and say to the victim. "Let me give you a hand. You look as if you are about to pass out." Then turning to those who were looking on, he would add: "Here folks, help me find a place for this person to lie down. He is ill."

If the "victim" had not actually passed out by this time, he generally did so when the fourth stooge approached him, grabbed him by the arm, and called, "Someone call a doctor quickly. This person needs attention."

I performed this experiment many times and never failed to make the "victim" temporarily ill. Finally the person chosen for the experiment, a man about thirty years of age, so completely passed out that he had to be hospitalized for a short time. The doctors finally convinced him that he had been the victim of an experimental hoax.

After that experience I tried no more experiments of this nature.

Convince the subconscious mind that you are ill, and it will go to work immediately to carry that conviction to its logical conclusion by actually making you ill. Hypochondria often produces the actual physical symptoms of illness, such as the breaking out of rash, or an upset stomach, or a headache, when the actual cause is nothing more than fear.

Inmates of the Ohio State Penitentiary formerly played a cruel joke on many of the newcomers to prison. The joke consisted of a committee of prisoners charging the newcomer with some imaginary infraction of the prison rules, and then condemning him to death. The victim was then blindfolded; his hands were tied behind him and his head was placed over a barrel, with several men holding him down tightly. Then one of the gang would ask if the knife had been properly sharpened. Someone would say, "Yes, I sharpened it myself right after we killed that last man. Here it is—now let him have it good and hard so he can't scream."

With that part of the ceremony finished, a comb would be roughly drawn across the victim's neck, quickly followed by spilling red ink over the neck. Then the victim would be turned loose, and everyone else would run for cover. Generally the first thing the victim did was to pull the blindfold from his eyes, and rub his neck with his hands, which of course led him to believe his throat had been cut, because there was the "blood" on his hands.

On one occasion a man thus victimized was so badly scared that he started running and screaming that he had been murdered. He had to be caught and subdued by prison guards, after which he was hospitalized for several days before he recovered from the shock, despite the fact he could plainly see his throat had not been cut.

The fear of sickness and the fear of physical pain are inborn fears, which come to the surface and take over at the slightest provocation. The fear itself, however, is always much worse than the thing which is feared. As Franklin D. Roosevelt said, during his first term in office, when the country was cursed by a stampede of fear, "The only thing we have to fear is FEAR itself." The truth might well be paraphrased in connection with the fear of dentistry, because modern dental techniques have practically removed all physical pain from every portion of the patient's body except one, *and that is the brain where his fear of pain exists, as a condition of mind he has created long before he sits in the dentist's chair.*

How to Reach and Influence the Subconscious Mind

The subconscious section of the mind receives activating influences from three sources: First, from all outside sources which convey influences to the individual through the five physical senses, including of course the words and deeds of others which come to one's attention. Second, through the sixth sense, which picks up thoughts released by others and passes them on to the individual by telepathy. Third, from the thoughts of the individual, including both the thoughts which are deliberately sent to the subconscious in the form of aims, plans, or desires, and *random thoughts which the individual indulges in without particular plan or purpose.*

Random, careless, negative thoughts occupy the minds of most people, and such thoughts produce undesirable circumstances, because they are picked up by the subconscious and acted upon. The subconscious does not differentiate between negative and positive thoughts, but accepts and acts upon one type as quickly as upon the other.

Here then is the reason why most people are in the classification of "failures." Most of their thoughts are of failure, and the subconscious mind carries them out to their logical conclusion.

Since the subconscious translates into their logical conclusion all thoughts which reach it—whether they are good or bad for the individual—it is clearly suggested that the way to put the subconscious mind to work for one in a helpful way *is by giving it definite orders as to what is desired.*

When it comes to giving orders to the subconscious

mind, there are some instructions which must be carried out to the letter:

(a) Write out a clear statement of that which you wish your subconscious mind to act upon, and set a definite time within which you wish action. Memorize this statement and repeat it to yourself, orally, hundreds of times daily, *especially just before going to sleep.*

(b) When you repeat your statement BELIEVE that it will be acted upon by your subconscious mind, *and see yourself already in possession of that which your statement calls for.* Close your statement by *expressing gratitude* for having received what you asked for.

(c) Before repeating your statement to your subconscious, work yourself into a high, intense state of emotional enthusiasm and joy because of your inner feeling that your request will be fulfilled. The subconscious acts almost instantaneously on thoughts which are *expressed in any state of high emotion,* either negative or positive. This last statement is highly significant. Please read it again and think about it.

How to Condition the Mind for Dentistry

We come now to the detailed instructions through which one may condition his mind for dentistry, and, by slight changes in the formula, the mind may be conditioned to meet any unpleasant circumstance which one contemplates, such as a major surgical operation, the loss of loved ones in death, etc. The instructions are as follows:

(a) Prepare the entire physical body for the contemplated operation by a three to seven days total fast, which *must* be conducted under the supervision of your physician. Two days prior to the beginning of the fast eat nothing but fresh fruits and drink only fruit juices, also omit *smoking* and *coffee*. You will be somewhat nervous during these two days but do not let that discourage you. At the end of the two days begin your fast and take nothing into your system except water with two or three drops of lemon juice added to each glass. Drink all the water you can—as many as a dozen or more glasses each day.

When the fast ends eat nothing the first day but one bowl of vegetable soup with no fat in it, and one slice of whole wheat bread, or toast. On the second day eat two bowls of vegetable soup and two slices of bread—one bowl in the forenoon and one in the afternoon. Starting the third day you may eat whatever you please as long as you *eat sparingly*. It is highly important that you come back to your normal eating habits gradually. In general, this is the procedure which should be followed, but every detail of it, including the number of days you should fast, *must be carefully checked by your physician before you begin your fast.*

The purpose of the fast, physically speaking, is to give your entire physical system, your stomach, your digestive organs, your eliminative system, your blood stream, an opportunity to take a vacation. The purpose of the fast, mentally speaking, *is to let you prove to yourself that you are the master of your stomach.* Once you have mastered your desire for food you will have little or no difficulty in mastering your fear of physical pain.

Still another purpose of the fast is that it *conditions your mind for easy communication with your subconscious mind.* During your fast your subconscious mind will be very sensitive to all influences around you, so beware of negative people and the discussion of negative subjects.

(b) Beginning on the first day of your fast, give yourself a treatment, through auto-suggestion, by repeating the following instruction to your subconscious mind at least once every hour, except when you are asleep, during your entire fast:

(1) I have complete confidence in _____, my dentist, in his skill, his character and his experience in dentistry.

(2) While my dental work is being performed by my dentist I shall completely disassociate my mind from it by keeping my mind on the thing I desire most in life, which is _____

_____

_____

(3) I desire my dental work to be done because it will add to my personal appearance and improve my physical health; and because I so desire it, I shall go through the operation as a welcome opportunity to prove to myself that my mind is stronger than the emotion of fear.

(4) I hereby direct my subconscious mind to take over my desire, as I have expressed it, and carry it out in every detail, and thus make my dental experience a magnificent interlude. Through this experience I shall make discoveries concerning the powers of my mind *with which I shall guide my entire future so as to get more joy out of life.*

These instructions are simple and understandable, but they will introduce you to a new way of life which may smooth your path in all your future experiences and human relations, as well as carry you through your dental operation without the slightest annoyance.

In these instructions I have introduced you to the most favorable condition under which you may give directives to your subconscious mind—during a fast. Under this condition your subconscious mind will be very alert and amenable to any influence which you may direct to it, or any influence which may get to it by your neglect to keep away from negative influences.

Now let us have a few words concerning the subject of fasting. Here are some of the benefits available through the habit of fasting, quite aside from the fact that fasting is an excellent method of preparing your subconscious mind to receive and carry out your directives:

(a) The habit of fasting, which should be carried on at least once or twice every year, tones up the entire physical body and aids it in building up bodily resistance to disease.

(b) Fasting provides an opportunity whereby one may easily break the habits of smoking and the drinking of coffee and alcoholic beverages. If you smoke or drink alcoholic beverages, as a habit, you will have to learn the habit all over again after you go through your fast, if you wish to smoke or drink again.

(c) Fasting brings one into very close relationship with one's spiritual powers, which is the major reason why directives given to the subconscious mind during a fast are so effective and operate so quickly.

(d) Fasting is an excellent habit for most neurotic and melancholic people who suffer with imaginary ailments, provided always that it is carried on under the supervision of a reputable doctor. Fasting is not child's play, and it never should be undertaken by anyone except by order of a doctor. Doctors in some schools of therapeutics successfully use fasting as a cure for many physical ailments.

(e) Fasting will not be difficult for those who follow the instructions I have here given, and keep their minds busily occupied during the fast, by giving directives to their subconscious minds. This is one of the major reasons for the habit of fasting because it opens wide the gate leading to the subconscious mind, during which any desired instruction may be given to the subconscious.

If you have never gone through a voluntary fast, you have a great treat coming to you when you first experience this practice. You may be slightly nervous the first two days, especially if you drink alcoholic beverages or coffee; but you will have an experience from there on such as you never had before. Recognition that you have mastered your appetite for food will give you a solid foundation on which you can, and perhaps will, develop mastery over many other things, such as poverty and failure and defeat and fear of every type.

Is not this promise worthy of an effort at fasting?

(f) While you are on your fast you will experience the return in memory of things which happened when you were a small child, and you will experience a feeling of self-confidence such as you perhaps never felt previously.

Some years ago, while I was associated with Bernarr Macfadden, I had an attack of influenza. After the attack seemed to have passed I had a recurrent spell of it, in a light form, about every two weeks. In speaking of this to Mr. Macfadden he said, "Why don't you go on a fast and starve that flu bug to death? Why keep on feeding it?"

Then he gave me instructions for fasting. I fasted for seven days, under the same instructions I have given here, with the result that the flu was completely eliminated, and more important still, I learned from that experience a system of body-conditioning which I have followed ever since—a system which has given me immunity from common colds as well as influenza.

My wife and I go on a fast together, at least annually. We make a sort of pleasant game out of the habit and get through it without inconvenience or discomfort. Two or more people fasting together, in a pleasant mental attitude, experience even greater benefits than if one were going through the experience alone.

When fasting in preparation for dental or surgical operations, the fasting should be ended at least two weeks before the operations begin. Meanwhile, after the fast is over your doctor should check your system thoroughly and make sure that your blood count, urinal, and heart tests are satisfactory. In some instances, one's diet, after a fasting experience, may need food supplements in the form of vitamins, *but these should be prescribed by your doctor,* not merely purchased on your own judgment. Quite often it happens that following the extraction of teeth, especially where full dentures are indicated, the gums do not heal satisfactorily and the dentist finds it necessary to prescribe food supplements in the form of vitamins.

One other suggestion concerning fasting: Do not engage in any heavy physical activities during the fast. Light housework or office work may be carried on during the fast without interruption, but over-exertions of every nature must be avoided.

There are many good books on the subject of fasting—a list of which is available at all public libraries. One of the best books on this subject I can recommend is *How To Fast,* by Bernarr Macfadden.

Mr. Macfadden so thoroughly conditioned his mind for the mastery of physical pain, through fasting some years ago, that he sat in a dentist's chair and had his teeth removed without the aid of any form of anesthetic. While this shows that pain can be mastered by mind control, I personally believe in anesthetics when it comes to a major surgical operation or the extraction of teeth.

The procedure I have here described could be applied as well to the mastery of poverty and the attainment of opulence, or financial prosperity, as to the conditioning of the mind for dental surgery. One would need only to change the statement of purpose to fit whatever objective was desired.

There are no limitations to the power of the mind save only those which the individual establishes for himself, or permits to be established by the influences outside of himself.

Truly, whatever the mind can *conceive* and *believe,* the mind can *achieve!*

Study well the three key words in the foregoing sentence because they epitomize the sum and the substance of this entire chapter.

Your success in the application of the mind-conditioning formula presented in this chapter will depend very largely upon the *mental attitude* in which you apply it. If you BELIEVE you will get satisfactory results, you will get them.

When you give directives to your subconscious mind, through the statement herein which was prepared for that purpose, you may hasten success *by repeating the statement in the form of a prayer,* and thereby place the entire power of your religious BELIEF back of your statement.

The word BELIEF is symbolic of a power that has no limitations within reason and we find evidence of its influence wherever we find people who have achieved noteworthy success in any calling.

Thomas A. Edison BELIEVED he could perfect an incandescent electric lamp, and that belief carried him successfully through the ten thousand failures before he got the answer for which he had been searching.

Marconi BELIEVED the ether could be made to carry the vibrations of sound without the use of wires, and that belief carried him through many failures until he was finally rewarded by triumph, and gave the world its first wireless means of communication.

Columbus BELIEVED he would find land in an uncharted portion of the Atlantic Ocean, and he sailed on and on until he found it, despite the threatened mutiny of his sailors who were not so blessed as he with the capacity for BELIEF.

Madame Schumann-Heink BELIEVED she could become a great opera singer, although her singing teacher had advised her to go back to her sewing machine and be content as a seamstress. Her BELIEF rewarded her with success.

Helen Keller BELIEVED she could learn to talk

despite the fact that she lost her use of speech, sight, and hearing, and her BELIEF restored her speech and helped her to become a shining example of encouragement to all people who are tempted to give up in despair because of some physical affliction.

Henry Ford BELIEVED he could build a horseless buggy that would provide rapid transportation at small cost, and despite the far-flung cry of "crack-pot" and the skepticism of the world, he belted the earth with the product of his BELIEF, and made himself immensely wealthy.

Madame Marie Curie BELIEVED that radium metal existed and gave herself the task of finding its source, despite the fact that no one had ever seen radium and no one knew where to start looking for it. Her BELIEF finally revealed the source of that precious metal.

When my son was born without ears, and I was told by the doctor who brought him into the world that he would be deaf all his life, I BELIEVED I had the power to influence nature to improvise a system of hearing for him. So I went to work through his subconscious mind and was rewarded when sixty-five percent of his natural hearing capacity was restored.

And when the time came for me to have all of my teeth extracted in preparation for dentures I BELIEVED—*nay, I knew*—I could go through the operation without the slightest discomfort. I KNEW because times without number I had seen the human mind master physical pain and all other unpleasant circumstances which people meet from time to time. I KNEW because I had learned from experience that my own capacity for BELIEF could remove all obstacles which got in my way, and set aside all of my self-imposed limitations.

The most profound truth known to man is the fact that man alone has been given the inexorable privilege of controlling and directing his own mind to whatsoever ends he may choose. All other creatures come into life bound by a pattern of "instinct" which they cannot change, and beyond which they cannot act. This distinguishing prerogative suggests that it is the key to man's control of his earthly destiny, and we know that neglect or failure to make use of this prerogative brings definite punishment in the form of misery, poverty, failure, defeat, illness, despair, and other negative states of mind. *We know also that the acceptance and use of this profound prerogative gives man the key to his own destiny.*

Here then is the supreme of miracles—THE POWER TO TAKE POSSESSION OF ONE'S OWN MIND AND TO DIRECT IT, SUCCESSFULLY, TO WHATEVER ENDS ONE MAY CHOOSE.

And another miracle of only slightly less distinction consists in the fact that along with this profound gift of the right of man to take possession of his own mind, there has been provided the source of power with which to make this gift limitless in man's achievements. This secondary miracle is the subconscious section of the mind through which man may contact and draw upon the universal powers of Infinite Intelligence.

The method by which one may contact Infinite Intelligence through the means of the subconscious mind is simple, it consists in the repetition of a thought, desire, or purpose, by bringing it into the conscious mind often and expressing it orally, in a state of high emotional feeling, thus enabling the subconscious mind to act upon it intelligently. The *SUBCONSCIOUS MIND WILL NOT ACT UPON ANY IDEA, PLAN, OR PURPOSE WHICH IS NOT CLEARLY EXPRESSED TO IT.*

In the preceding sentence you have a cue as to the major reason why so many people fail to get satisfactory results from their subconscious minds. Also you have the major reason why most people are failures instead of successes.

When you give directives to your subconscious mind, be definite and clearly state your desires, and you will not be disappointed, provided you emotionalize your directives with strong BELIEF that they will be carried out. *By this procedure the power which operates the Universe will be at your disposal!*